TRAIN
DRIVER'S
MANUAL

ABOUT THE EDITOR

COLIN MAGGS is one of the country's foremost railway historians and an authority on the Great Western Railway. He is the author of nearly 100 railway books, and in 1993 he received the MBE for services to railway history. He lives in Bath.

Praise for Colin Maggs:

A History of the Great Western Railway
'Comprehensive and full of charming anecdotes'
CHRISTIAN WOLMAR
'A very readable account of God's Wonderful Railway'
BBC WHO DO YOU THINK YOU ARE MAGAZINE

The GWR Bristol to Bath Line
'Well researched and authoritative' *BRISTOL EVENING POST*

The Branch Lines of Dorset
'Absorbing, entertaining and well researched'
THE RAILWAY OBSERVER

The Branch Lines of Somerset
'Lively and informative' *THE BATH CHRONICLE*

TRAIN DRIVER'S
MANUAL

Edited by
COLIN MAGGS

AMBERLEY

Acknowledgement is due to Alan Norrington for very helpful advice.

First published 2014

Amberley Publishing
The Hill, Stroud,
Gloucestershire, GL5 4EP

www.amberley-books.com

British Library Cataloguing in Publication Data.
A catalogue record for this book is available from the British Library.

ISBN 978-1-4456-1680-3 (paperback)
ISBN 978-1-4456-1695-7 (ebook)

Typesetting and Origination by Amberley Publishing.
Printed in Great Britain.

CONTENTS

INTRODUCTION

Until about fifty years ago every schoolboy wanted to be a steam engine driver. It seemed so easy and exciting; you just opened the regulator and off you sped.

Well it was not quite that simple – you had to know how to release the brakes, and in addition to those on the engine, there were those on the tender. Even before releasing the brakes there were other vital jobs to be done.

A machine needs lubrication. A locomotive is a very big machine and needs lubrication in many places, so takes quite a time to prepare and some of the places to oil are in awkward and sometimes dirty spots.

Perhaps a fireman's job is simpler – you just throw a shovelful of coal into the fire. Well, you could, but to make your job easier by burning less coal, you have to know exactly where and when to place it. You do not want to have a good head of steam if you are going to descend a long gradient, neither do you want to be sparing with the coal when you are faced with a long, steep climb.

Then there is the need to keep an eye on the water level because an engine needs to take on water more often than coal. Should the water level in a boiler become dangerously low, a fusible plug in the top of the firebox will melt and bring shame on the neglectful fireman. So, being a steam locomotive man requires more than meets the eye – it needs years of training.

The years of apprenticeship, after a medical examination including a colour-blindness test, are spent firstly as an engine cleaner, because going round cleaning the locomotive makes a lad familiar with all its parts. In addition to cleaning the visible portions of an engine, he may be required to clean the boiler tubes with a long, T-shaped scraper and, if a tube was completely blocked, free it with a dart – a spear-like tool.

In due course he is given easy firing duties and learns how to handle a shovel and place coal in the part of the fire where it is needed. He is also taught how to clean the ash pan and smoke box, both dusty and unpleasant jobs. Before a cleaner can become a passed cleaner and act as a fireman he is required to be able to name the principal parts of an engine, know the relevant rules and regulations and be familiar with a fireman's duties and responsibilities. These include seeing that sufficient coal and water are available, that the lamps are in working order and tools correctly positioned. When a passed cleaner had achieved 328 days of firing (a year minus rest days), he was paid at the firing rate regardless of whether he was firing or cleaning.

For a fireman to become a passed fireman, which meant that he could be called upon to drive an engine, he was required to take an examination consisting of about four days of practical and theoretical tests. He learned in his own time at mutual improvement classes led by senior footplatemen in their own time.

The tests required him to name every part of an engine and be able to take down one side of the motion, so that in the event of a locomotive becoming disabled, it could be put into a condition that would enable it to be worked back to a shed, for often it was possible to nurse a failed steam engine back to a depot. This is one great advantage of a steam locomotive, whereas a failed diesel engine needs depot facilities for repair.

A fireman was also tested on his knowledge of signalling, rules and regulations, making out reports, oiling and his ability to change a water gauge glass. He was allowed three attempts at this exam and if he failed a third time he was not allowed to go on firing, but was taken off the footplate and put on labouring – but as one driver put it, 'You had to be pretty dim to fail.'

A driver's examination was in two parts: in the shed and out on the road. At the shed, the inspector might 'go round the wheel', asking which cylinder port was open to live steam and which port open to exhaust. The four quarters, the four angles and the fore and back gear made thirty-two port openings to be memorised. This knowledge was considered essential to enable a driver to identify a valve or piston defect and thus report correctly. A driver was also tested on how he would deal with other defects which might occur. A driver would also probably be asked a question about making trimmings for conveying lubricating oil to the working surfaces.

There were three types of worsted trimmings: plug, tail and pad. A plug trimming is used for rotating and oscillating parts with sufficient motion to splash oil over the end of a tube into which the plug is fixed. This type of trimming is made by wrapping several strands of worsted lengthwise over a piece of twisted wire to form a plug which fits comfortably into the tube.

A tail trimming is used to lubricate parts such as piston rods and axle box guides and made of the same material as the plug variety, but the strands are sufficiently long to fit into a siphon tube suspended into an oil box in order to siphon the oil from the reservoir to the area needing lubrication. Pad trimmings are used for die blocks, expansion link pins and axle journals, the pads being saturated with oil each time the locomotive is prepared. Subsequently they gently lubricate during the engine's working.

A driver generally learned a road when he had previously fired over a route having learned the gradients, position of signals, speed restrictions

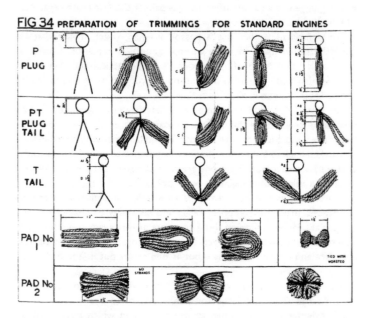

FIG 34 PREPARATION OF TRIMMINGS FOR STANDARD ENGINES

and the stopping points at various stations so that in bad weather, or at night, he would know exactly where he was. Listening to lineside noises indicated his whereabouts — for instance, travelling through a cutting would sound different from being in the open. A good, helpful driver would impart such information to his fireman. Firemen's and drivers' duties were arranged in links. A fireman began in a shunting link and moved up through the goods and passenger links, but when made a driver he had to start again in a shunting link and might be in his fifties before regularly driving an express passenger train.

I

WHAT A FIREMAN SHOULD KNOW

A general rule in order to maintain an even fire is to place on coal 'little and often'. If a fire is too thick, the air needed for combustion cannot get through, while if the fire is too thin, there is the danger of a hole developing and cold air spoiling steam generation and perhaps even causing leaks in the firebox.

A watch has to be made for clinker as it can prevent air coming through to maintain the fire, while if the ash pan is full, it can choke the grate. Should the fire and ash pan become clogged with clinker and ash, and efforts with pricker and dart make little effect, it may be necessary to stop, shovel out the clinker from the firebox and clean the fire.

A fireman must be aware of the water level, especially on inclines. On a steep rise the water falls towards the back of the boiler, making the gauge give a high reading, but if beyond the summit there is a steep fall, the water rushes to the front of the boiler and if the water is not sufficiently high this could lead to the fusible plug melting. (These are lead plugs screwed in and if overheated, the lead melts and steam smothers the fire.) Thus it is essential to have the water level to the top nut of the gauge when ascending, to ensure that it is still above the bottom nut when the boiler tips forward for the descent.

In the early days of locomotives, feed water was delivered to the boiler by a pump driven from an axle or crosshead, which meant that water could only be delivered to the boiler when the locomotive was moving. Thus if an engine was stationary for a long period and water in the boiler was getting low, it had to run up and down the track to replenish the boiler.

The problem was overcome by using an injector using either live or exhaust steam to force-feed water into the boiler. An injector's great advantage is that it can be used whether the engine is moving or stationary, though the exhaust steam injector only works with the regulator open.

Water is obtained from a water column provided at engine sheds or at the ends of platforms at major stations. Side tank engines have both tanks linked by pipe so that only one need be filled as the water automatically runs into the other, though if a fireman wishes to take on the maximum amount of water, he raises the filler cap on the other tank to check the height of the water as it can take some time to pass through to the other tank. Air is displaced by the water escapes through a vent.

Out on the road a fireman might have been able to take water from troughs. He lowered his scoop and then when the tank was approaching the full mark, the scoop raised. The scoop was moved by a screw, the design of which is inherently slow in action, and to avoid drenching the first coach the scoop had to be started to be raised well before the gauge registered full. It was a task which required considerable experience. As an aid, lineside boards marked the beginning and end of a trough.

A skilful fireman knows when his driver will require more steam and when he will require less, and so in theory none of his efforts in raising steam will escape through the safety valves. However perfection is not always obtainable, particularly if there is an out-of-course stop, so when the regulator is closed, an injector is often put on to prevent the safety valves blowing off and thus wasting steam.

When a locomotive is returned to a shed, disposal consists of removing char from the smoke box, and ash and clinker from the firebox. If the engine is fitted with a rocking, or drop grate, this is a relatively easy procedure, but if it is not so fitted, then one of two methods can be adopted: either using a long shovel and throwing the clinker out of the cab through the doorway, or lifting four or five fire bars with gigantic pincers and raking the ash and clinker through the gap into the ash pan. The fire bars are then replaced using the pincers. With either method, the contents of the ash pan need to be raked out, but this is unnecessary with a hopper ash pan.

A Fireman's Main Running Controls

Steam and water valves for live steam injector.
Steam and water valves for exhaust steam injector.
Blower. (Shared with the driver.)
Damper levers.

QUESTIONS FOR ENGINEMEN

1. *Q.*—Is it a fact that engine cleaners have ample opportunity during the course of their daily work to make themselves acquainted with the general arrangement of steam railway locomotives?

A.—Yes, and it is noticeable that although these locomotives are of various types, they all have features which are common, such as, for example, frames, cylinders, wheels, firebox, boiler, safety valves. There are, of course, differences in the sizes, number and positions of the cylinders, and of the wheels.

2. *Q.*—The locomotive stock owned by the Company is classified according to the power and purposes of its units. Could you identify the class to which a locomotive belongs?

A.—Yes, the class is shown by a small number and letter on the side of the cab, but the size of the boiler and the arrangement of the wheels readily indicate the purpose, and suggest the power, of the locomotive.

3. *Q.*—Where are the cylinders of the locomotive usually placed?

A.—Two-cylinder engines have the cylinders side by side under the smokebox, between the main frames (e.g., Class 4 Freight) or one outside each main frame (e.g., Class 5 Mixed Traffic).

A three-cylinder engine has one inside between the frames, and one outside each of the frames.

LOCOMOTIVE WHEEL ARRANGEMENTS.

ARRANGEMENT.	TYPE.	EXAMPLE.
	O-4-O	SADDLE TANK ENGINE. NO. 7000 (STANDARD.)
	2-4-O	PASSENGER TENDER ENGINE. NO. 20002 (M.R.)
	2-4-2	PASSENGER TANK ENGINE. NO. 10910. (L.& Y.)
	4-4-O	PASSENGER TENDER ENGINE. STANDARD COMPOUND. NO. 900.
	O-4-4	PASSENGER TANK ENGINE. NO. 6400. (STANDARD.)
	4-4-2	PASSENGER TANK ENGINE. NO. 2110. (L.T.& S.)
	O-6-O	FREIGHT TENDER ENGINE. NO. 3835. (STANDARD.)
	2-6-O	MIXED TRAFFIC ENGINE. NO. 2700. (STANDARD.)
	O-6-2	FREIGHT TANK ENGINE. NO. 2270. (N.S.)
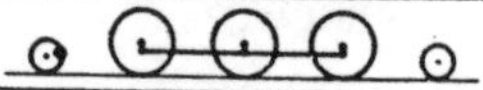	2-6-2	PASSENGER TANK ENGINE. NO. I. (STANDARD.)
	4-6-O	"ROYAL SCOT" PASSENGER ENGINE. NO. 6100. (STANDARD.)
	O-6-4	PASSENGER TANK ENGINE. NO. 2000. (M.R.)
	2-6-4	PASSENGER TANK ENGINE. NO. 2300. (STANDARD.)
	4-6-2	"PRINCESS ROYAL" PASS. ENG. NO. 6200. (STANDARD.)
	4-6-4	PASSENGER TANK ENGINE. NO. 11110. (L.& Y.)
	O-8-O	FREIGHT TENDER ENGINE. NO. 9500. (STANDARD.)
	2-8-O	FREIGHT TENDER ENGINE. NO. 8000. (STANDARD.)
	O-8-2	FREIGHT TANK ENGINE. NO. 7870. (L.N.W.R.)
	O-8-4	FREIGHT TANK ENGINE. NO. 7930. (L.N.W.R.)
	O-IO-O	BANKING ENGINE. NO. 2290. (M.R.)

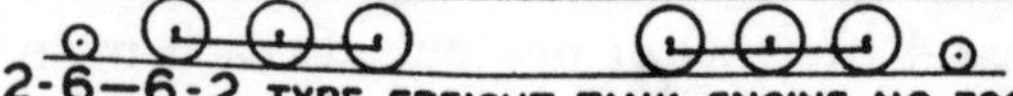

2-6—6-2. TYPE FREIGHT TANK ENGINE. NO. 7987. (STANDARD.)

FIG. I

L.M.S.
DRAWING OFFICE
DERBY.
D.D. 2988.

POSITION OF ENGINE HEAD LAMPS

ALL LONDON MIDLAND AND SCOTTISH ENGINES, WHETHER WORKING OVER THE LMS. OR OTHER COMPANIES' LINES, AND THE ENGINES OF OTHER COMPANIES WORKING OVER THE L.M.S. LINE, MUST UNLESS INSTRUCTIONS ARE ISSUED TO THE CONTRARY, CARRY WHITE HEAD LIGHTS ARRANGED AS UNDER:—

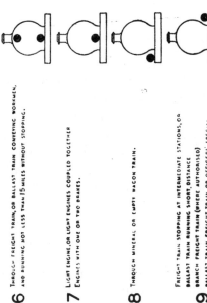

1 EXPRESS PASSENGER TRAIN, OR BREAKDOWN VAN TRAIN GOING TO CLEAR THE LINE, OR LIGHT ENGINE GOING TO ASSIST DISABLED TRAIN, OR FIRE BRIGADE TRAIN.

2 ORDINARY PASSENGER TRAIN, OR BREAKDOWN VAN TRAIN NOT GOING TO CLEAR THE LINE.
BRANCH PASSENGER TRAIN (WHERE AUTHORISED)
RAIL MOTOR OR MOTOR TRAIN WITH ENGINE LEADING
(WHEN RUNNING WITH DRIVING COMPARTMENT LEADING RAIL MOTORS OR MOTOR TRAINS WILL CARRY THE HEADLAMP ON THE SAME BRACKET AS USED FOR THE TAIL LAMP)

3 PARCELS, NEWSPAPERS, FISH, MEAT, FRUIT, MILK, HORSE, OR PERISHABLE TRAIN, COMPOSED OF COACHING STOCK

4 EMPTY COACHING STOCK TRAIN, FITTED FREIGHT, FISH OR CATTLE TRAIN WITH THE CONTINUOUS BRAKE IN USE ON NOT LESS THAN ONE-THIRD THE VEHICLES.

5 EXPRESS FREIGHT OR CATTLE TRAIN WITH THE CONTINUOUS BRAKE ON LESS THAN ONE-THIRD THE VEHICLES, BUT IN USE ON FOUR VEHICLES CONNECTED TO THE ENGINE INDICATED BY ✱ IN THE WORKING TIME TABLES
EXPRESS FREIGHT OR CATTLE TRAIN NOT FITTED WITH THE CONTINUOUS BRAKE, OR WITH THE CONTINUOUS BRAKE IN USE ON LESS THAN FOUR VEHICLES.

6 THROUGH FREIGHT TRAIN, OR BALLAST TRAIN CONVEYING WORKMEN, AND RUNNING NOT LESS THAN 15 MILES WITHOUT STOPPING.

7 LIGHT ENGINE, OR LIGHT ENGINES COUPLED TOGETHER
ENGINES WITH ONE OR TWO BRAKES.

8 THROUGH MINERAL OR EMPTY WAGON TRAIN.

9 FREIGHT TRAIN STOPPING AT INTERMEDIATE STATIONS, OR BALLAST TRAIN RUNNING SHORT DISTANCE
BRANCH FREIGHT TRAIN (WHERE AUTHORISED)
BALLAST TRAIN, FREIGHT TRAIN, OR OFFICERS' SPECIAL REQUIRING TO STOP IN SECTION OR AT INTERMEDIATE SIDING IN SECTION.

SHUNTING ENGINES WORKING EXCLUSIVELY IN STATION YARDS AND SIDINGS, MUST, WHILST IN THOSE SIDINGS, CARRY ONE RED HEAD LIGHT AND ONE RED TAIL LIGHT.
THE LAMPS MUST BE CARRIED IN POSITION DAY AND NIGHT.
WHEN A TRAIN RUNNING ON THE LMS RAILWAY IS WORKED BY TWO ENGINES ATTACHED IN FRONT OF THE TRAIN, THE SECOND ENGINE MUST NOT CARRY HEAD LAMPS.

NOTE:— LOCAL EXCEPTIONAL ARRANGEMENTS WILL REMAIN IN FORCE

FIG.2

A four-cylinder engine has two inside and two outside the frames.

————

4. *Q.*—Is there any method which can be recommended as being particularly helpful in becoming familiar with the Book of Rules and Regulations ?

A.—Yes, the whole of the rules should be carefully read, and those concerning enginemen frequently re-read ; the best method is to make a list of these and make a pencil mark opposite each of them, so that afterwards whenever the book is opened and a marked rule is seen, it is instantly recognised as one of those which must be memorised.

When supplements are issued containing alterations of the rules, the change should be noted and read after which the original rule or part thereof in the Rule Book which is altered should be deleted and the amendment gummed in over it.

Drivers and Passed Firemen are supplied with copies of the General or Sectional Appendices to the Working Time-tables, which also contain orders and instructions liable to alteration or amendment. Firemen and Passed Cleaners firing have access to these on request to their Driver.

Special attention must be paid to the posted notices and circulars exhibited at the Motive Power depots.

————

5. *Q.*—Can the list of rules which are of particular importance to enginemen be readily compiled ?

A.—Yes, the subjects are easily found by reference to the Index to the Rule Book ; for instance, under the letter " F " in the Index a number of rules for firemen are quoted, and under the letter " S " are some referring to both hand and fixed signals, and under the letter " E " are references to rules containing the word " engine," and by making use of these references a complete list is compiled without difficulty. See Section No. 13.

6.   *Q.*—Why is it imperative that you should carefully observe the speed restrictions at curves and other places to which they apply?

A.—Because these speeds are very carefully calculated by the Engineers, and are the highest allowable over the particular sections.

7.   *Q.*—What details on the tender call for attention?

A.—The coal must be kept safely stacked ; the tools secured ; the brake and water scoop screws oiled and scoop handle secured by chain, and the cover over the tank filling hole in place, to prevent dirt and coal falling in, thereby causing injector trouble.

8.   *Q.*—Do you realise that in this brief series of questions and answers it is not possible to review all the incidental responsibilities of your vocation as engine driver or fireman?

A.—Yes, and I am alive to the advantage of familiarising myself with the information and instructions contained in the Rule Book and its Appendices in the Working Time-table, and also in the notices posted at the Depots.

I can also gain further information from Mutual Improvement Class Meetings and the M.I.C. page in the L.M.S. magazine.

9. *Q.*—What steps do you take to ensure that, in a case of emergency, you would unhesitatingly act upon the instructions contained in the Rule Book?

A.—From time to time in the course of my work I ask myself what I would do in the event of certain mishaps occurring.

10. *Q.*—What three aims should always be to the forefront of a driver's mind?

A.—Safety; punctuality; efficiency.

SECTION 2.

ON THE SHED—ENGINEMEN'S DUTIES

(*a*) Engine Preparation.
(*b*) Engine Disposal.

11. *Q.*—Mention some of the duties of a Fireman after he has signed on, read his notices and joined his engine on the Shed.

A.—His first duty would be to examine and test the water gauges (see Fig. 3 and 3a); notice the steam pressure, and if this is sufficient at once test both injectors. If there is insufficient steam pressure he should at once proceed to level the fire in the box, and

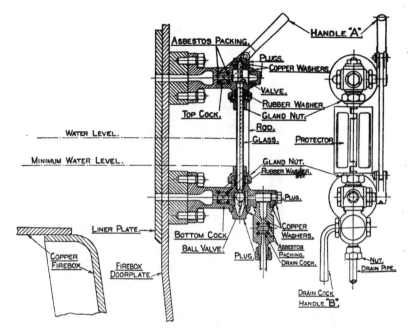

Labels in figure:
ASBESTOS PACKING.
HANDLE "A".
PLUGS.
COPPER WASHERS.
VALVE.
RUBBER WASHER.
GLAND NUT.
TOP COCK.
ROD.
WATER LEVEL.
GLASS.
PROTECTOR.
MINIMUM WATER LEVEL.
GLAND NUT.
RUBBER WASHER.
PLUG.
LINER PLATE.
COPPER FIREBOX
FIREBOX DOORPLATE.
BOTTOM COCK.
BALL VALVE.
PLUG.
COPPER WASHERS.
ASBESTOS PACKING.
DRAIN COCK.
NUT.
DRAIN PIPE.
DRAIN COCK HANDLE "B".

TO TEST GAUGE COCKS.

1. SHUT TOP AND BOTTOM COCKS BY PULLING HANDLE "A" UNTIL IT IS POINTING DOWNWARDS HALFWAY BETWEEN THE HORIZONTAL AND VERTICAL.

2 OPEN DRAIN COCK BY PULLING HANDLE "B" UPWARDS UNTIL HORIZONTAL, AND WATER SHOULD DISAPPEAR.

3. OPEN TOP AND BOTTOM COCKS BY RAISING HANDLE "A" SLOWLY UNTIL IT IS POINTING UPWARDS HALF WAY BETWEEN THE HORIZONTAL AND VERTICAL IN ORDER TO BLOW THROUGH, AND CLOSE AGAIN.

4. SHUT DRAIN COCK BY TURNING HANDLE "B" DOWNWARDS.

5. OPEN TOP AND BOTTOM COCKS WITH HANDLE "A" UNTIL IT IS POINTING UPWARDS HALF WAY BETWEEN THE HORIZONTAL AND VERTICAL AND WATER SHOULD RISE TO LEVEL.

WATER GAUGE COCKS.

L.M.S.
DRAWING OFFICE.
DERBY.
DD.2997.

FIG.3

WATER GAUGE COCKS

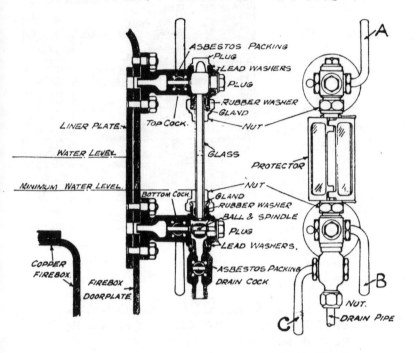

TO TEST GAUGE COCKS

1 SHUT TOP COCK AND BOTTOM COCK BY PULLING HANDLES 'A' AND 'B' BACKWARDS UNTIL HORIZONTAL

2. OPEN DRAIN COCK BY PULLING HANDLE 'C' BACKWARDS UNTIL HORIZONTAL AND WATER SHOULD DISAPPEAR.

3. BLOW THROUGH TOP COCK BY OPENING WITH HANDLE 'A' AND CLOSE AGAIN.

4. BLOW THROUGH BOTTOM COCK BY OPENING WITH HANDLE 'B' AND CLOSE AGAIN.

5. SHUT DRAIN COCK WITH HANDLE 'C'.

6. OPEN TOP COCK AND BOTTOM COCK WITH HANDLES 'A' AND 'B' AND WATER SHOULD RISE TO LEVEL.

FIG. 3 A.

commence to build it up in order to raise steam without delay, so that the injectors can be tested as early as possible.

If the state of the fire is entirely unsatisfactory or the steam pressure and water level excessively low, no time should be lost in notifying the Driver and the Foreman, who will then, if necessary, be able to provide another engine without incurring any delay.

It is the Fireman's duty to draw the tools and equipment from the stores, clean, fill and trim the head lamps, gauge lamp and the hand lamp. He must inspect the Detonator canister to note whether the lid is properly sealed in position, and if the wire is broken he should obtain a sealed canister from the Stores. When using a coal of clinkering nature he must obtain a supply of limestone or broken firebrick (according to which is available at the Depot) and spread this evenly over the firebars as early as possible after the fire has been levelled out.

The Fireman should also satisfy himself that the smokebox is properly cleared of char, and afterwards must see that the smokebox door is securely fastened up, taking care to wipe the faces of the door joint clean of char before closing it. He must also be particular to sweep the front platform and foot framing clear of all loose char, and sand, which will be liable to blow about into the motion, and in any ease, present an untidy and slack appearance.

The sand boxes and the container of the sand gun must be filled, and finally the Fireman must pay special attention to the position of the fire-irons and coal on the tender, and must see that all are properly stowed in accordance with instructions.

————

12.   Q.—Are any special precautions necessary when cleaning the water gauges ?

A.—Yes. It is important not to remove the gauge glass protector before releasing all pressure from the gauge glass, and also not to re-apply pressure to the gauge glass before the protector has been replaced in position. When opening the gauge frame taps to re-apply pressure to the gauge glass after cleaning, open the taps only very slightly at first with the drain tap still open in order to blow a small quantity of steam through the glass to warm it up. If pressure is applied suddenly to the gauge glass, the rapid heating may fracture the glass. Always examine the gauge glass protectors to see that they are in good condition, and the catches sound.

If the gauge glass is dirty outside and requires washing, always use a cloth soaked in warm water ; a cloth soaked in cold water will probably cause the gauge glass to crack if applied to it.

————

13.   Q.—In what position should the gauge glass protector be fixed ?

A.—With the brass plate containing holes facing the boiler back plate.

————

14.   Q.—How should the fire be prepared ?

A.—The coal in the firebox should be spread evenly over the entire grate, and a few shovels of small coal sprinkled around the sides of the box to start the fire burning vigorously. The damper should be opened slightly and the blower applied sufficiently to promote proper combustion at this stage.

Leave the freshly applied coal to burn up, obtain a supply of limestone or clean broken firebrick, if required, and spread this over the grate before putting on any further coal. The lumps of coal should be broken so that the largest put on the grate is about twice the size of a man's closed fist. This exposes to the action of the fire a greater surface than would be exposed if much larger lumps were used.

Now commence to build up the fire, putting on a small quantity of coal at a time, firing round the sides of the box, and avoid placing coal in the centre of the grate unless any holes exist in the fire there. If coal is fired to the centre of the grate dense volumes of smoke will be produced, and this is to be avoided at all times.

Continue firing thus at intervals, giving each charge of coal time to ignite properly before introducing more, until the desired amount of coal is in the firebox and well alight.

———

15. *Q.*—Name a few of the Driver's chief duties after signing on duty to prepare an engine in the Shed.

A.—After signing on duty the Driver should read the current notices and sign for those which require it. He will obtain his job card and any special instructions affecting his workings for the day.

Upon reaching his engine he will see the gauge frames tested, and satisfy himself that the lead plugs and tubes are tight. At the same time noting the condition of the fire and the steam pressure.

He should see both the injectors tested, and himself test the vacuum brake and the sanding gear so that if any defects are disclosed he can have them attended to in good time and avoid a late start.

Before leaving the Shed the water scoop should be tested and oiled, and great care taken to see that the scoop is in the " Up " position to avoid any damage being done when the engine is moved, and the Driver must satisfy himself that the coal and fire-irons are properly and safely stored on the tender.

---

16. *Q.*—What points should be borne in mind when oiling up an engine ?

A.—The Driver should have a definite system in mind and always work to it. It is best to commence at the same point dealing with the various parts methodically, and always in the same order, for in this way there is less possibility of overlooking any oiling points. The efficient Driver will also be at pains to become acquainted with the differences in layout in the various classes of engines with which he will have to deal in the course of his duties.

---

17. *Q.*—Some Drivers before setting back on to a Passenger train put a drop of oil on the tender buffer faces. Is this good practice ?

A.—Yes, because it prevents chafing of the buffers and lessens the jolts that may be transmitted by the tender to the first coach of the train.

18. *Q.*—When preparing an engine which is to steam heat the train to be worked what test should be made?

A.—See that the flexible hosepipe and connections are in good order. Then test the carriage warming apparatus by first opening the cock on the tender end (or the cocks at each end of a tank engine so fitted), open the steam valve and blow out all condensed water in the apparatus, close the cocks and see that the correct steam heating pressure can be obtained.

If the regulation pressure cannot be obtained or is exceeded with a train of any length the matter must be fully reported on a repair card.

————

19. *Q.*—Describe the Fireman's chief duties prior to and during the disposal and stabling of an engine.

A.—Towards the end of the run the fire must be levelled in the box, and worked down as low as possible to avoid coming on the Shed with a large amount of unburned coal on the grate. Experience will soon indicate the best time to commence working the fire down, but the aim should be to run on to the Shed with the fire as low as possible.

Arriving on the Shed at a modernised Depot the first duties will be to take coal from the Mechanical Coaling Plant and water before proceeding on to the Ashpit.

On the Ashpit the Fireman will empty the smokebox of char and clean or lift out the fire according to his instructions upon the matter. Whilst he is performing these duties the Driver will be making his examination of the engine. Finally, the ashpan must be raked out making full use of the slaking pipe, and left quite clear of ashes, after which all dampers and the firehole doors are to be tightly closed.

The Driver will have ascertained whether the engine is to be turned, and where it is to be stabled, and it should be placed in the Shed on the road indicated.

The Fireman should now collect, check and return tools and equipment to the Stores. If any item has been lost or damaged he should inform his Driver who will report the fact when signing off, and the Fireman should draw the Storesman's attention to the discrepancy when handing over the equipment. Before leaving the engine inside the shed, the boiler should be filled with water to a height of three-quarters of gauge glass.

———

20. *Q.*—Why is it necessary to close the dampers and firehole door after the fire has been lifted ?

A.—Because if this were not done cold air would enter the hot firebox and set up severe contraction stresses in the plates, stays and tubes, which would thus be liable to damage and leakage. For the same reason the blower jet must not be used after the fire has been lifted, and when necessary to move the engine under its own steam with the fire out, the engine must be worked as lightly as possible to reduce the quantity of cold air which would be drawn through the empty firebox and tubes.

———

21. *Q.*—Are any special precautions necessary when taking coal at a Mechanical Coaling Plant ?

A.—Persons operating any kind of machinery must take certain elementary precautions in their own interest and that of others in the vicinity. Enginemen should take every opportunity to make themselves familiar with the different types of coaling plants and their controls. During coaling, stand well clear of the tender and coal chutes, and the Fireman should on no account get on to the tender to break lumps or clear a jam without first intimating clearly to the person at the control what his intentions are. **Avoid overcoaling the tender which leads to excessive spillage.** When the tender is overcoaled there is a risk of the coal falling off and causing accidents to the staff.

——————

22. *Q.*—What are the special points to bear in mind when operating a mechanically propelled turntable?

A.—In addition to the usual precautions taken to prevent movement of the engine, the propelling mechanism of the turntable must be handled carefully.

If this is the vacuum tractor type, the starting valve must be opened slowly to reduce shock to the gearing, and care must also be taken to see that the catches are out before the tractor is started, and the table must never be stopped by forcing the catches in. The tractor must never be used as a brake to stop the table by reversing. In all cases the tractor should be shut down at such a point that the table will roll to rest in the desired position of its own accord. Finally to provide plenty of power always use the large ejector to operate the tractor.

23. *Q.*—What indicates a careful and competent Driver in the simple matter of setting an engine on a turntable or opposite a water column ?

A.—The competent Driver is alert and knows exactly where to stop, having previously noticed what part of that type of engine comes opposite to a certain part of the turntable or to a line side mark as the case may be, so that he is able to stop quickly and easily in the desired position without waste of time in setting back.

Engines must always be taken slowly on to and off turntables and brought to rest easily to avoid straining the mechanism, and structure of the turntable. During the operation of turning, the hand brake must be screwed hard on, the steam brake released, reversing lever in mid gear position, and the cylinder drain cocks open.

———

24. *Q.*—Why should hand operated turntables always be pushed round and never pulled ?

A.—Because when pushing, a man operating the table is behind the push bar so that if he should slip or fall the table will move away and leave him clear. A man pulling on the bar, however, might be injured if he slipped and fell because the moving bar would pass over him.

———

25. *Q.*—Describe how a Driver should examine his engine.

A.—He should begin always at one particular point and proceed round the whole engine and tender in a systematic way. If he goes from one part to another at random, it is probable that confusion will result and some important items may be overlooked.

2

WHAT A DRIVER SHOULD KNOW

Before starting a locomotive a driver should go round his machine and oil or grease the various bearings, fill the lubricators and look out for any defects. In the cab he should test the brakes, sanding gear and injectors. When booking on he is required to read the Weekly Notice listing such things as temporary speed restrictions, water columns out of action or a diversion from the normal route.

When coupled to a train, unless it is unfitted, a full continuous brake test is carried out to ensure that the brake is operating throughout. Immediately the guard gives the 'Right away' by showing his green flag, the vacuum brake handle is moved to the big ejector position to blow off the train's brake blocks. The signal should be checked to ensure that the road ahead is actually clear. The whistle is then blown to warn all and sundry in the neighbourhood that the train is about to move.

Before actually starting, the cylinder cocks must be opened as steam entering a cold cylinder turns to water and could cause the cylinder to burst.

The engine should be set in full forward gear, that is about 75 per cent cut-off, and the regulator opened. Should the train be heavy, the rails greasy or the train on a severe curve of gradient, sand may need to be applied to prevent slipping which is wasteful of coal and damaging to both machine and rails. Using a 75 per cent cut-off allows very little expansion of the steam and thus is wasteful, so as soon as possible the cut-off should be reduced. As speed rises the reverser is eased to 45 and then 25 per cent cut-off. When running fast, it should be between 15 and 25 per cent of the stroke.

Although it is standard practice that a locomotive should normally be driven on full regulator and power reduced or increased by altering the cut-off, this does not apply to a slide-valve locomotive, which requires the regulator to be closed before altering the cut-off. However, some drivers prefer using the regulator rather than the cut-off as the regulator is easier to move.

Although the instruction is to blow the whistle before moving, a crafty driver can save a few seconds by opening the regulator and then blowing the whistle. The instruction is still obeyed because there is always a pause between opening the regulator and the steam actually moving the pistons. If the track is level, another few seconds can be saved by blowing off the brakes before the 'Right away' and holding the train by means of the engine's handbrake, or the locomotive-only steam brake.

Should an engine fail to produce sufficient steam for the job in hand, matters may be improved if the injector is temporarily turned off. This offers two advantages: firstly that no cold water enters the boiler and secondly the saving of steam used to operate that injector. When saturated steam contacts metal surfaces in pipes and cylinders it cools and when steam condenses back to water, a vacuum is formed, so a 'push' on a piston is converted to a 'pull'. If closing the injector fails to produce steam-saving results, another trick is to increase the cut-off to produce a stronger blast which may clear the tubes of ash and thus increase the flow of oxygen to the fire.

If saturated steam is additionally heated in a superheater, it becomes superheated and its moisture content turned to additional steam, so no losses occur through condensation.

Three-link couplings for freight stock have the advantage that a relatively low-powered engine can haul a heavy goods train. Because more effort is needed to start a train moving than to keep it in motion, it means that with three-link couplings an engine can start from a standstill hauling just one wagon, then as the links tighten, two wagons and so on.

Buck-eye couplings weld an engine and train into one solid mass, but a driver having spring buffers and screw couplings on his engine can use this to his advantage. If, just before a train comes to rest at a stop, the driver applies more brake power to the engine wheels than to the train, he ensures that the coupling between engine and train is slightly slack. This means that the engine can be set in motion slightly before the rest of the train.

Having started a train, it is useful to know how to stop it. When a full emergency application of the continuous vacuum brakes is made, the vacuum gauge needle drops from 21 inches (or 25 on a GWR locomotive) to zero. Three things then happen: the hiss of air to the ejector; the grinding of blocks on the wheels and the feeling of retardation. As speed decreases, the brake handle is moved to recreate a vacuum which will ease the pressure on the brake blocks and adjustments are made to bring the train to a stand at the appointed spot.

When running, the small ejector is usually left on to maintain the vacuum against leakages, while the large ejector is used to blow the brakes off before starting. GWR engines have a vacuum pump to maintain the vacuum when running.

One driver attempted to close the regulator, found that nothing happened and that his engine continued at full speed. All was not lost. He kept his head and controlled the engine by means of the reverser and brake, even managing to balance his engine on the turntable.

Should an engine slip to a standstill on a gradient, as long as the train is not in the vicinity of a catch point, the driver can set back for a few yards with his rear sanders open and then when the train starts, open the forward sanding gear to maintain the adhesion.

If this fails, there are the options of either seeking assistance from another engine, or dividing a train, taking the first portion to the next station and placing it in a siding before returning for the remainder of the train. The latter method is not usually used for a passenger train.

When a locomotive is left unattended the handbrake should be applied and the reverser left in mid-gear, in other words, halfway between full forward and full reverse, and the drain cocks open.

A Driver's Main Running Controls

Regulator.
Reversing lever or wheel.
Cylinder cock operating lever.
Whistle cord.
Brake valve.
Sanding control.
Blower. (Shared with the driver.)

26. *Q.*—Suppose the examination is started at the leading end on the Driver's side, how would the Driver proceed?

A.—In this case the Driver would pass down alongside the engine to the rear of the tender, across the back and return to the front end along the Fireman's side. He would then go under the engine, and proceed thus right through to the rear of the tender.

———

27. *Q.*—What is the best position in which to set an engine for examination underneath?

A.—Engines with two inside cylinders, which includes four-cylinder engines, are best set with the inside big ends on the bottom angles, and three cylinder engines should be set with the inside big end on the bottom quarter. In all cases the regulator must be properly closed, and hand brake hard on, the reversing lever in mid gear position, and the cylinder cocks open.

———

28. *Q.*—Name a few of the parts requiring special attention in the course of the Driver's examination.

A.—The Driver should be particular to report all blows and should ascertain by test if necessary during his examination from whence they originate. He should note whether the valve spindles and piston rods are properly lubricated and not dry. All slide bar bolts, big and little end cotters should be examined. Symptoms of defects noted whilst running should be reported in full.

————

29. *Q.*—What points should be observed in reporting any details on the engine that may be defective?

A.—The headings on the Repair Card should be fully and clearly filled in and as much detail as possible given concerning the part reported. It must be remembered that the fitter who will do the repair may find the engine out of steam when he gets to it. The report should, therefore, convey to him as far as possible what is wrong so that he will be able to go straight to the defective part and not waste time examining parts that are working correctly.

————

30. *Q.*—What is the procedure when there are no known defects?

A.—If there are no known defects a "No repairs" card must be made out.

SECTION 3.

COMBUSTION

31. Q.—Of what does the combustible matter in coal consist?

A.—The principal combustible constituent of coal is carbon, but it also contains substances known as hydro-carbons and traces of sulphur, etc.

32. Q.—What do you understand by hydro-carbons?

A.—A hydro-carbon is a chemical compound of the gas hydrogen and carbon. In gas coals the hydro-carbons are the chief light-producing constituents.

33. Q.—Do you understand what is taking place when the coal burns?

A.—When coal burns the carbon and other combustible constituents combine chemically with oxygen from the air, in the process of which a considerable amount of heat is given out.

34. Q.—Where is the necessary supply of oxygen obtained from to burn the coal in a locomotive firebox?

A.—It is obtained from the air drawn in through the dampers and the firehole door by the action of the blast in the smoke box.

35. Q.—What is formed when carbon burns?

A.—If the combustion is complete a colourless gas called carbon dioxide is formed. Each lb. of carbon so burned produces approximately 14,000 B.T. units of heat.

——————

36. Q.—If the combustion is not perfect, what happens then?

A.—In that case the whole of the carbon would not be consumed and a colourless and highly poisonous gas called carbon monoxide would be produced. Each lb. of carbon so imperfectly burned only produces 4,500 B.T. units of heat.

If a further supply of oxygen was then introduced the carbon monoxide gas would ignite and burn with a pale blue flame, giving out a further considerable quantity of heat to form carbon dioxide gas. In the absence of a further supply of oxygen the carbon monoxide gas would escape up the chimney unburned and the available heat in it would be lost. This represents a loss of 69 per cent. of the available heat.

——————

37. Q.—How are the hydro-carbons in the coal burned?

A.—They combine with the atmospheric oxygen to form carbon-dioxide and water, which the heat of the firebox converts into steam, and which is carried away with the other flue gases up the chimney by the draught.

If the combustion is not complete due to lack of sufficient oxygen some of the carbon will be left in a free state, and will pass away up the chimney where it will appear in the form of smoke.

——————

38. Q.—What is the effect of clinker if it forms in the fire?

A.—If clinker is allowed to form in large quantities it will block the air spaces in the grate and prevent the air supply admitted through the dampers from passing through the fire which in consequence will become dead, refusing to burn properly, so that the steaming of the boiler will be affected.

In this event it will be necessary to break up and dislodge the clinker by using the straight dart to lift it from the firebars and the pricker to clear out the air spaces in the grate.

———

39. *Q.*—Is there anything that can be done to prevent the formation of clinker?

A.—Incorrect firing and mismanagement of the dampers tends to accelerate the formation of clinker.

The best safeguard is to spread about half to one bucketful of broken clean firebrick or (if supplied) limestone, over the grate before the fire is built up during engine preparation. These materials tend to collect the clinker round themselves as it forms, and by so doing preventing it from adhering to the firebars.

———

40. *Q.*—A very large quantity of air will be required to ensure proper combustion of the whole fire in a locomotive firebox. How is this large quantity of air supplied to the fire?

A.—As previously stated it is drawn n by the blast and enters the firebox through the dampers upwards through the firegrate and also through the firehole door, to the top of the fire. Most of the L.M.S. engines have hollow firehole doors which allows of a certain amount of secondary air to be admitted even when the doors are closed.

41. Q.—Is it necessary to admit air by both the firehole door and the dampers ?

A.—Yes, practically always. The air drawn through the firegrate is necessary to maintain the bed of fuel incandescent, whilst the air admitted by the firehole door serves to complete the combustion of the gases liberated from the glowing coal below.

————

42. Q.—Can it be assumed from this then that so long as there is plenty of air being admitted through the dampers and the firehole door that the best results will be obtained ?

A.—Certainly not. All air admitted to the firebox over and above the quantity necessary for complete combustion of the coal will pass through the boiler unchanged except that it will become heated in its passage. This means that the surplus air robs useful heat from the fire which could otherwise be used to produce steam, and furthermore the loss of this heat from the fire lowers the temperature of the firebox.

————

43. Q.—Since it is wasteful to admit excess air to the firebox what effects would follow if insufficient air were admitted ?

A.—If insufficient air is allowed to enter the firebox complete combustion of the coal is impossible because there will not be enough oxygen to combine with all of the carbon in the fuel, and some of the carbon will pass through the tubes unburned, to appear at the chimney in the form of smoke. There is also the risk that the carbon consumed will only be burned to carbon monoxide and that the hydro-carbon vapours will also escape unburned from the chimney, giving rise to a serious heat loss in addition to the production of smoke.

————

44. *Q.*—How is it possible to judge then when the correct amount of air is being admitted to the firebox to give perfect combustion?

A.—One method is to set the dampers and firehole door so that a clear exhaust is obtained, but that when the firehole door is closed very slightly smoke appears at the chimney.

Another method is to adjust the dampers and firedoor so that there is just a perceptible discolouration of the exhaust at the chimney. This method has the advantage that there is something visible to watch, and there is no chance of admitting excess air, which, of course, will give a colourless exhaust, but will reduce the firebox temperature.

In either case, if combustion is almost perfect, each shovel of coal fired will be accompanied by a dash of smoke from the chimney, lasting perhaps one or two seconds.

————

45. *Q.*—What is the brick arch for?

A.—The brick arch serves several useful purposes. It protects the tube plate and the tube ends from the direct flame from the fire. During intervals of firing when the firebox temperature falls, the brick arch radiates heat which tends to prevent rapid fluctuations in the tube plate temperature.

The brick arch also promotes thorough combustion of the gaseous products of the fuel by lengthening their path from the fire grate to the tube plate, and at the same time acting in conjunction with the firehole deflector plate it causes these burning gases to be intimately mixed with the supply of top air admitted to the firebox through the firehole door.

---

46. *Q.*—What is Controlled Firing?

A.—For a very long time Firemen have been instructed to fire " Little and Often," but unfortunately that wise maxim has been too frequently ignored. In order that this principle should be better understood it is proposed to use the term " Controlled Firing." This term means the same as " Little and Often " but carries it a little further by stating how little and how often.

Controlled Firing can be described as firing at equal time intervals, as it lays down that a *definite number* of shovels of coal well broken up should be fired at short regular intervals and the time between firings should not be altered by reason of speed or gradient.

The actual number of shovels of coal fired will, of course, depend on the work the engine has to do and this will be determined by experience, but as the firing is done on a *time* basis, variation in speed and gradient will not affect the rate of firing.

An engine pulling a train up a bank will burn more coal per mile than on the level but as it travels more slowly uphill the coal burnt per minute need not vary.

Controlled Firing saves coal because it is never added at such a rate that the gases it gives off cannot be burnt by the air passing over the fire from the firedoor. It also prevents waste due to excessive firing before or on a rising gradient.

It is better to use the coal on the grate as a reservoir of heat to be drawn on when the engine is working hard, than to make a large increase in the rate of firing, bringing down the temperature in the firebox and causing black smoke. In Controlled Firing the reservoir is built up again on the down gradient by continuing to add coal at the regular two-minute intervals.

The number of shovels of coal to be fired will depend upon the work the engine has to do and the Fireman's guide to this will be the maintenance of his boiler pressure on the gauge. Controlled Firing, of course, does not dispense with the Fireman's knowledge of the road, when to use the injector and when to cease firing, but it lays down sound principles which, when combined with his road experience, enables him to fire his engine when running with efficiency and economy.

---

47. Q.—Are there any conditions under which a fire should not be maintained as thin as it is possible for it to burn?

A.—Yes, when the firegrate is small the action of the blast is liable to be keener and would tend to pull a thin fire into holes. Under such conditions a rather thicker fire should be carried.

---

48. Q.—How should the coal be put on during firing?

A.—This varies with different grates, depending upon the shape and slope, etc., but in all cases the person firing must aim to prevent the formation of holes in the fire. Generally it is advisable to maintain the fire thicker at the corners and sides, and to avoid placing much coal in the centre which will cause smoke.

In a sloping grate do not fire much to the front except to prevent the formation of any holes because the coal will shake down forwards and feed the front of the box, and it is usually advisable to keep the back corners well filled. (See Figs. 4 and 5.)

---

49. *Q.*—Why must the Fireman be so particular to avoid the formation of holes in the fire?

A.—Because if there is a hole in the fire the air naturally tends to pass in at this spot because this is the easiest path for it. The rush of air through the hole will lift particles of glowing fuel carrying them through the tubes and out of the chimney whilst the remainder of the fire will become dead and the firebox temperature will fall, due to imperfect combustion.

---

50. *Q.*—Can the condition of the fire be examined whilst the engine is working?

A.—Yes, a rapid examination of the state of the fire over the entire grate can be made by resting the shovel blade on the firehole mouthpiece and using it to direct a stream of air on the part of the fire it is desired to examine. By moving the shovel blade it is possible to direct the air stream to each part of the fire in turn, and to examine the whole fire.

The Fireman should endeavour at all times to avoid the use of fire-irons since excessive use of these tends to accelerate the formation of clinker and disturbs the fire.

COMPLETE COMBUSTION

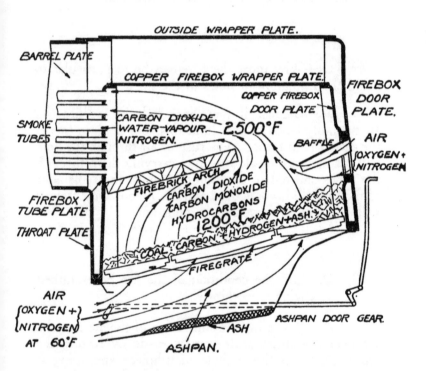

SECTION OF FIREBOX SHOWING THAT GASES ARE FORMED AND THAT TEMPERATURES OF UPWARDS OF 2500°F. ARE OBTAINED DURING THE COMPLETE COMBUSTION OF COAL.

FIG 4.

INCOMPLETE COMBUSTION

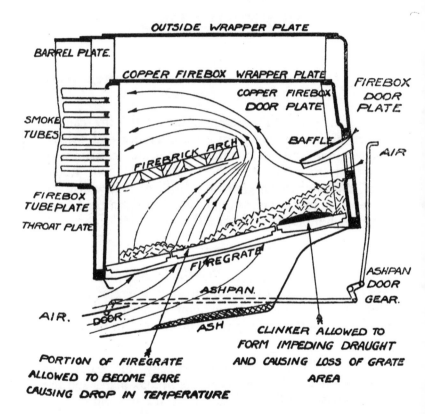

SECTION OF FIREBOX SHOWING EFFECTS OF
MISMANAGEMENT OF FIRE.

FIG 5.

MEASUREMENT OF HEAT AND PROPERTIES OF STEAM SUPERHEATING

---

51. *Q.*—Do you know what temperatures are attained by the fire in a locomotive firebox?

A.—Yes. The temperature of the fire can be gauged approximately from its appearance and colour. Red, orange and yellow flames indicate temperatures ranging from 1,000° to 1,200° Fahr. At about 1,800° Fahr. the fire will be glowing a brilliant red, whilst the fierce white furnace glow under good working conditions indicates temperatures from 2,000° to 2,500° Fahr.

---

52. *Q.*—Why is it then that the firebox plates do not become damaged by exposure to such a degree of heat, which is above the melting point of steel and copper and far above the melting point of the lead in the fusible plug?

A.—Because of the capacity of water for absorbing heat. So long as all the firebox plates and the tubes exposed to the radiation from the fire and contact with the hot flue gases are covered on the opposite side with water, the heat passed to the metal is absorbed immediately by the water on the opposite side with the result that the temperature of the plates and tubes remains low and is in fact only a few degrees higher than that of the water inside the boiler.

53. *Q.*—Would it be a serious matter then if any part of the firebox or heating surface was not covered by water?

A.—Yes, if any part of the firebox or tubes were to be uncovered by water even for a few seconds, the plates would become overheated. When this occurs through low water the firebox crown sheet is affected first, and the lead plugs fitted to it will fuse, allowing steam to fill the firebox and to smother the fire. Even if the lead plugs fuse, however, there is a risk that the firebox crown sheet will be scorched and damaged, and to drop a lead plug is therefore, a very serious matter.

———

54. *Q.*—What is steam?

A.—Steam is an invisible gas produced by the evaporation of water upon application of heat. When steam is produced in a closed vessel so that it is retained in contact with the water from which it has been produced it is known as saturated steam.

If the steam is led away from the water and heated still further at constant pressure, in a separate vessel or chamber, the steam is said then to be superheated.

———

55. *Q.*—Is there any connection between the temperature and pressure of steam?

A.—In the case of saturated steam, yes. If steam is produced from water in a closed vessel it will accumulate over the water, and produce a pressure within the vessel, and it is found that there is a corresponding temperature for every recorded pressure. As the pressure increases, the temperature of the steam also rises.

56. *Q.*—Since the temperature of steam appears to rise automatically as the pressure is increased, what is the object of superheating steam?

A.—To supply it with a greater quantity of energy in the form of heat than it would possess naturally at that particular pressure, consequently a given weight of superheated steam will be capable of developing more power in the cylinders than the same weight of saturated steam at equal pressure.

---

57. *Q.*—What practical benefits arise from the use of superheated steam?

A.—The application of further heat to the steam during superheating causes it to expand so that less weight of superheated steam is required to fill the cylinders at each working stroke than would be the case if saturated steam at equal pressure were used.

Since it takes a pound of water to produce a pound of steam, it follows that if superheating enables the cylinders to do their work on a lower weight of steam, a saving of water and coal will result.

A further advantage in favour of super-heating is that sufficient heat can be retained in the steam after expansion behind the piston to prevent condensation taking place within the cylinders.

---

58. *Q.*—What is the special characteristic of steam as a working agent?

A.—Steam has the property of storing up a vast amount of energy in the form of heat and it does work by giving up this heat as it expands inside the cylinders. This is generally referred to as the expansive property of steam.

---

59. *Q.*—How is the expansive property of steam made use of in a locomotive?

A.—Steam stored in the boiler at high pressure is admitted to the steam chest by way of the Regulator valve, internal steam pipe, superheater (if fitted) and external steam pipe. From the steam chest distribution to the cylinders is controlled by the valves which in turn admit the steam to the cylinders, retain it therein, and release it to exhaust after it has expended its energy on the pistons.

Whilst the steam is enclosed within the cylinder it expands behind the moving piston exerting a gradually diminishing pressure upon it as it does so. This portion of the working cycle in the cylinder is known as the " expansion period."

The Driver can control the length of the expansion period in the cylinders within limits set by the valve gear by use of the reversing lever. As the lever is " notched up " the "admission period " is reduced in length and the expansion " period " correspondingly increased.

This is what is known as " expansive working " and results in a lower consumption of steam per stroke than would be obtained if live steam were admitted for the entire stroke and the expansive powers of the steam disregarded.

SECTIONAL VIEW

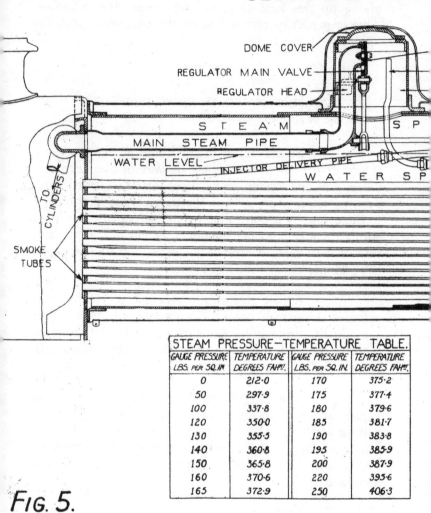

DOME COVER

REGULATOR MAIN VALVE

REGULATOR HEAD

S T E A M   S P

MAIN STEAM PIPE

WATER LEVEL

INJECTOR DELIVERY PIPE

W A T E R   S P

TO CYLINDERS

SMOKE TUBES

STEAM PRESSURE—TEMPERATURE TABLE.

GAUGE PRESSURE LBS. PER SQ.IN	TEMPERATURE DEGREES FAHRT.	GAUGE PRESSURE LBS. PER SQ. IN.	TEMPERATURE DEGREES FAHRT.
0	212.0	170	375.2
50	297.9	175	377.4
100	337.8	180	379.6
120	350.0	185	381.7
130	355.5	190	383.8
140	360.8	195	385.9
150	365.8	200	387.9
160	370.6	220	395.6
165	372.9	250	406.3

FIG. 5.

OF BOILER

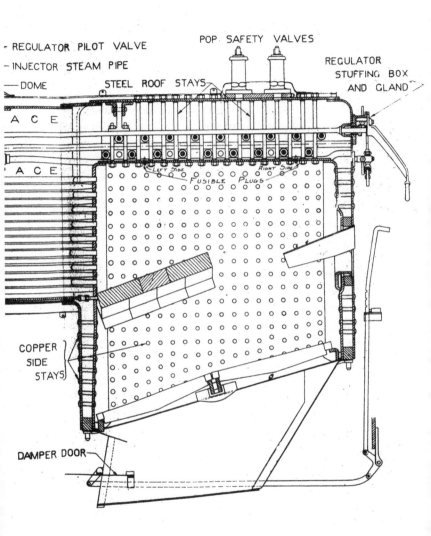

REGULATOR PILOT VALVE

INJECTOR STEAM PIPE

DOME

STEEL ROOF STAYS

POP SAFETY VALVES

REGULATOR STUFFING BOX AND GLAND

A C E

A C E

LEFT SIDE

RIGHT SIDE

FUSIBLE PLUGS

COPPER SIDE STAYS

DAMPER DOOR

THE LOCOMOTIVE BOILER

60. *Q.*—Describe the principal parts of the loco-motive boiler.

A.—The principal parts of the locomotive boiler are the steel shell, which includes the boiler barrel and the firebox wrapper plates and the smokebox tube plate, the inside firebox which is generally made of copper and the fire tubes leading from the inner firebox to the smokebox tube plate within the barrel. The inner firebox is secured to the wrapper plates by over a thousand stays passing through the water spaces which surround the inner firebox on all sides except the bottom, which is closed by the foundation ring. When a super-heater is fitted this consists of a number of large flue tubes placed above the ordinary fire tubes within the boiler barrel ; these flues house the superheater element tubes through which the steam has to pass on its way from the regulator valve to the steam chest. (See Fig. 7.)

The fire box may be of the long narrow type which is carried between the frames, or it may be of the shallow wide type as on the " Princess Royal " engines, in which case it is spread over the frames and supported by a pair of small carrying wheels under the trailing end. The wide type of firebox is employed in cases where a large grate area is necessary.

61. *Q.*—Name four of the most important boiler fittings.

A.—The four chief boiler fittings are the safety valves, the water gauges, the regulator valve and two injectors.

62. *Q.*—Where would you expect to find these fittings mounted on a locomotive ?

A.—The safety valves are mounted usually over the firebox crown where the bulk of the steam is generated. The water gauges are mounted on the boiler back plate in the cab, the regulator valve is generally fitted inside the boiler at the highest point above the water level, and when a steam dome is fitted the regulator will be mounted in this. Sometimes the regulator is fitted in the smokebox and steam is led to it by an internal pipe running from the highest point inside the boiler shell where steam is driest. The injectors, of which there are two, may be mounted behind the footsteps or if they are of the " lifting type " on the boiler back plate inside the cab.

———

63. *Q.*—Mention two types of slide pattern Regulator valves used on the L.M.S.

A.—The two most common types of Regulator valve are the vertical slide valve type as fitted to the old standard engines (see Fig. 6) and the horizontal slide valve regulator as used on the Taper boiler engines. This latter type of regulator is employed with only slight modification for both smokebox and dome mounting. (See Fig. 8.)

———

64. *Q.*—Describe briefly how the slide pattern Regulator valve operates.

A.—The vertical slide valve regulator is so called because the valve face is arranged vertically. Usually the face has four ports, two small ones for starting purposes, and two large ports for normal running.

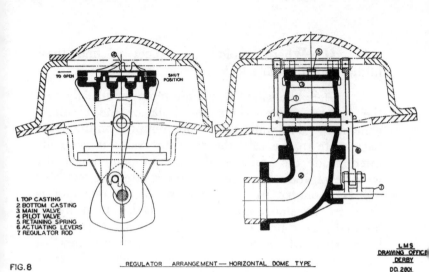

1 TOP CASTING
2 BOTTOM CASTING
3 LIVE VALVE
4 PILOT VALVE
5 RETAINING SPRING
6 ACTUATING LEVERS
7 REGULATOR ROD

REGULATOR ARRANGEMENT — HORIZONTAL DOME TYPE

FIG. 8

L.M.S
DRAWING OFFICE
DERBY
DD. 2801

1. REGULATOR HANDLE
2. MAIN STEAM VALVE FOR STEAM MANIFOLD.
3. LIVE STEAM VALVE TO EXHAUST STEAM INJECTOR.
4. LIVE STEAM PIPE TO INJECTOR.
5. EXHAUST STEAM INJECTOR.
6 AUXILIARY STEAM PIPE FROM STEAM CHEST TO INJECTOR.
7 EXHAUST STEAM PIPE TO INJECTOR.
8. WATER FEED PIPE TO INJECTOR.
9. DELIVERY PIPE FROM INJECTOR TO BOILER.
10. OVERFLOW PIPE FROM INJECTOR.
11. WATER CONTROL GEAR FOR INJECTOR.
12 STEAM VALVE TO LIVE STEAM INJECTOR
13 LIVE STEAM PIPE TO INJECTOR.
14. LIVE STEAM INJECTOR
15. WATER FEED PIPE TO INJECTOR.
16. DELIVERY PIPE FROM INJECTOR TO BOILER.
17. OVERFLOW PIPE FROM INJECTOR.
18. WATER CONTROL GEAR FOR INJECTOR.
19. STOP VALVE TO EJECTOR STEAM VALVES
20. SMALL EJECTOR STEAM VALVE.
21. LARGE EJECTOR STEAM VALVE.
22 COMBINED, LARGE & SMALL EJECTOR
23. VACUUM GAUGE
24. DRIVER'S BRAKE VALVE
25. TRAIN PIPE
26 STEAM BRAKE PIPE
27. STEAM BRAKE CYLINDER LUBRICATOR
28. DRIP VALVE FOR TRAIN PIPE.
29 TRAIN PIPE CONNECTION TO TENDER.

30 STEAM PIPE TO ENGINE BRAKE CYLINDER
31. STEAM BRAKE PIPE CONNECTION TO TENDER.
32. STOP VALVE TO CARRIAGE WARMING REDUCING VALVE.
33. CARRIAGE WARMING REDUCING VALVE.
34 CARRIAGE WARMING PRESSURE GAUGE.
35. CARRIAGE WARMING HOSE PIPE CONNECTION TO TENDER.
36. WATER GAUGE COCKS.
37. STOP VALVE TO SANDING VALVE.
38. STEAM SANDING VALVE.
39. SAND PIPE TO TRAILING WHEELS.
40. SAND PIPE TO LEADING & DRIVING WHEELS.
41. STEAM VALVE FOR BOILER PRESSURE GAUGE.
42. BOILER PRESSURE GAUGE.
43. WHISTLE VALVE
44. WHISTLE HANDLES
45. BLOWER VALVE.
46. STEAM VALVE FOR SAND GUN.
47. SAND GUN HAND OPERATING WHEEL.
48. STEAM PIPE FROM STEAM CHEST TO SAND GUN.
49. SAND HOPPER FOR SAND GUN.
50. CONTINUOUS BLOW DOWN VALVE.
51. STEAM PIPE FROM STEAM CHEST TO BLOW DOWN
52 BLOW DOWN PIPE TO TENDER.
53. REVERSING SCREW HANDLE.
54 CYLINDER DRAIN COCK HANDLE
55. DRIVER'S SEAT.
56. FIRE HOLE DOOR.
57 COAL WATERING COCK
58 ASHPAN HANDLES.

L.M.S.
DRAWING OFFICE,
DERBY,
DD 2986.

FIG. 9

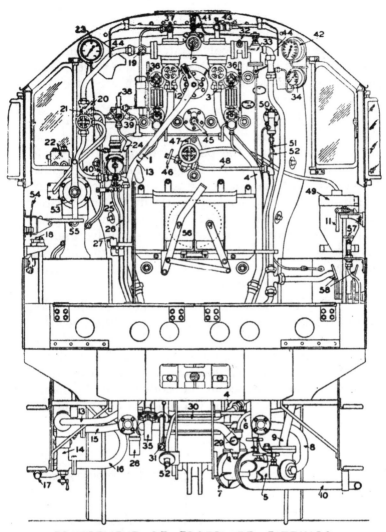

ARRANGEMENT OF FOOTPLATE FITTINGS.

Resting on the valve face is the main valve which has four ports cut in it, and the starting or pilot valve rests in turn on top of the main valve. The pilot valve usually has two ports which are used for starting purposes.

The sequence of movements when operating this regulator is as follows :—First movement of the regulator handle lifts the pilot valve till the two small starting ports are open. Further movement of the handle then moves both the pilot valve and main valve together, which action opens the large ports in the main valve and closes the starting ports. During closing, the pilot valve is first moved down over the main valve into its normal position, and then both valves are brought back together to their original position, closing the main steam ports as they move down.

The independent movement of the pilot valve is obtained by the use of a circular fitted hole for the operating pin in the pilot valve and an elongated hole or slot in the main valve, the result being that the latter does not move till the pin has travelled a distance corresponding to the clearance in the slotted hole, a distance which is made equal to the lap and port opening of the pilot valve.

————

65. Q.—How does the horizontal slide type regulator work?

A.—The principle of these regulators is exactly the same as the vertical pattern described in the previous question, the only differences being of arrangement to suit the horizontal mounting.

A main valve and pilot valve are employed, but the operating pin in this case engages with slots formed in the raised sides of the valves, the slots in the main valve being wider than the diameter of the pin by an amount equal to the lap and port opening of the pilot valves.

---

66. Q.—What other fittings are there that require live steam from the boiler?

A.—In the majority of engines there would be the steam brake or the vacuum ejectors, the blower, steam sanders, whistle, carriage warming apparatus, and possibly one or more sight feed displacement type lubricators, and on the taper boiler engines there are the atomisers for assisting the lubrication of the piston valves.

---

67. Q.—You have not referred to the sand gun or the continuous blowdown fitting; do not these use live steam from the boiler?

A.—No. These fittings are both operated by steam taken from the steam chest so that they can only be operated when the engine is working.

---

68. Q.—From what part of the boiler is the steam usually taken to work the auxiliary fittings?

A.—From the dome when one is fitted and in the case of old standard engines a separate pipe would be taken from the dome to feed each injector, the brake, blower, sanders and the C.W.A. On the taper boiler engines the auxiliary fittings, with the exception of the blower, are supplied with steam from a steam manifold mounted on the back of the firebox, the manifold casting taking steam from the highest point in the boiler through a single pipe ; steam can be shut off from the manifold by a plug in the centre, the blower in this case having a steam pipe of its own, making a total of two pipes as against a minimum of six in the case of other engines.

---

69. Q.—What is the registered working pressure of a locomotive ?

A.—The registered working pressure of a boiler is the steam pressure for which it has been designed, and it is indicated by a metal tablet secured to the firebox backplate, and also by a red line on the face of the steam pressure gauge. If the pressure at which the safety valves lift does not correspond to within 5 lbs. either way on the pressure gauge to the registered pressure the matter must be reported.

---

70. Q.—Does escape of steam from the safety valves entail loss to the Company ?

A.—Yes, it represents a waste of labour, coal and water which can very largely be avoided by careful management of the fire by the Fireman.

For example, a Class 5 Mixed Traffic engine blowing off steam continuously at the safety valves for five minutes will entail a waste amounting to 70 lbs. of coal and 60 gallons of water.

---

71. Q.—What depth of water should be maintained in the boiler as a good working level ?

A.—To maintain the gauge glass about half to three-quarters full is best. This provides a good depth of water over the firebox, and at the same time leaves plenty of steam space, so that priming will be unlikely.

---

72. *Q.*—Will any ill effects result from having too much water in the boiler?

A.—Yes, too high a water level is bad because it restricts the steam space and leads to priming which in time will lead to such troubles as damaged cylinders and pistons, bent connecting rods and possible difficulty in releasing the vacuum brake, and injector troubles due to water getting into the steam supply to these fittings.

---

73. *Q.*—Where is the water delivered into the boiler?

A.—Either into the front end, by pipes passing within the boiler along each side (see Fig. 6) or, in the case of taper boiler engines, through top clacks on to trays inside the top of the boiler, which distribute the water over the water surface near the smokebox tube-plate. (See Fig. 7.)

---

74. *Q.*—Water is delivered into the boiler either by means of pumps or by injectors, the latter being the most commonly used. Explain the working principle of an injector. (See Fig. 10.)

A.—A jet of steam emerging at high velocity from the steam cone is brought in contact with the cold feed water which is admitted around the tip of the steam cone. Partial condensation of the steam jet takes place,

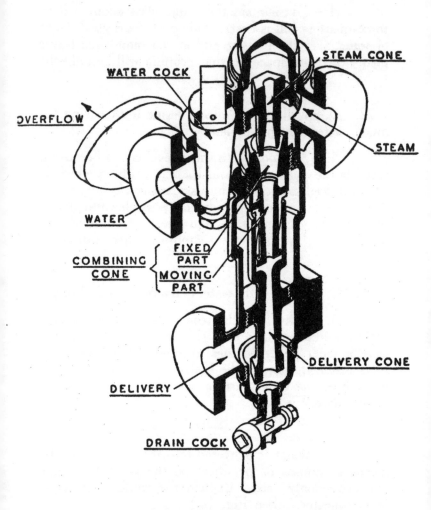

STEAM CONE

WATER COCK

OVERFLOW

STEAM

WATER

COMBINING CONE { FIXED PART / MOVING PART }

DELIVERY CONE

DELIVERY

DRAIN COCK

STANDARD INJECTOR

FIG.10

a partial vacuum is formed, and the water is drawn forward at considerable speed into the wide end of the converging combining cone. Passage through this cone completes condensation of the steam producing a high vacuum and the water emerges from the small end of the cone at greatly increased velocity. The water jet then jumps the overflow gap and enters a diverging cone known as the delivery cone.

The shape of this cone causes the speed of flow to be quickly and considerably reduced, which process converts the energy of motion in the water jet into pressure energy at the outlet end of the delivery cone.

The pressure developed in this way at the delivery end of the injector exceeds the boiler pressure sufficiently to enable the feed water to lift the clack against steam pressure and enter the boiler.

The vacuum developed in the combining cone when the injector is working is used to hold a movable section of the cone up against the front portion giving the effect of a continuous cone. If the action of the injector is interrupted or the water jet upset, the vacuum in the cone is replaced by pressure, the moving section is forced away from its seating, and any surplus steam and water escapes through the gap so formed to the overflow outlet. When the pressure has been relieved the working vacuum rapidly re-establishes itself and the injector will then start again.

In some types of injector the moving cone is replaced by a hinged flap forming one side of the combining cone. In this case the flap is forced open when the injector flies off. Injectors incorporating such devices are known as automatic restarting injectors.

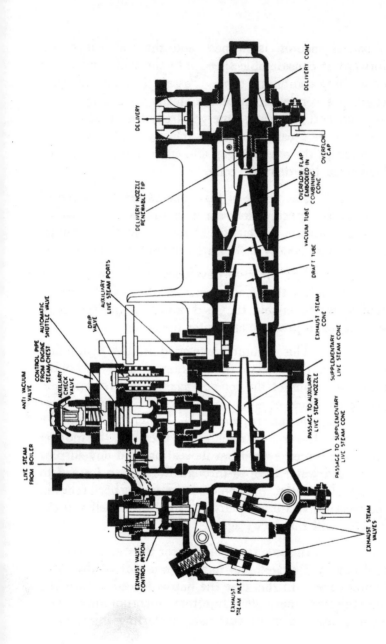

EXHAUST INJECTOR
CLASS 'H'

FIG.II

DELIVERY

DELIVERY CONE

DELIVERY NOZZLE
RENEWABLE TIP

OVERFLOW FLAP
EMBODIED IN
COMBINING CONE

OVERFLOW
CAP

VACUUM TUBE

DRAFT TUBE

EXHAUST STEAM
CONE

SUPPLEMENTARY
LIVE STEAM CONE

AUTOMATIC
SHUTTLE VALVE

CONTROL PIPE
FROM ENGINE
STEAM CHEST

AUXILIARY
LIVE STEAM PORTS

DRIP
VALVE

ANTI VACUUM
VALVE

AUXILIARY CHECK
VALVE

LIVE STEAM
FROM BOILER

PASSAGE TO AUXILIARY
LIVE STEAM NOZZLE

PASSAGE TO SUPPLEMENTARY
LIVE STEAM CONE

EXHAUST VALVE
CONTROL PISTON

EXHAUST STEAM
VALVES

EXHAUST
STEAM INLET

58

75. *Q.*—What is the best system of using the injectors ?

A.—Where two live steam injectors are fitted, they should be used in turn to keep both in good working order.

———

76. *Q.*—What is the purpose of the exhaust injector?

A.—To provide an economical method of injecting water into the boiler by utilising exhaust steam from the blast pipe for the purpose. Exhaust steam also heats the feed water, so that a very hot feed is obtained. For best results the injector should always be at work when the engine regulator is open, the feed being regulated by the handle on the Fireman's side of the cab. The hottest feed is obtained with this handle in the minimum position.

———

77. *Q.*—Explain the working of the exhaust injector.

A.—With the engine regulator open, the exhaust injector works with Exhaust steam, together with a small supply of Supplementary live steam. With the engine regulator shut, auxiliary live steam replaces the Exhaust steam, the supply of supplementary live steam continuing. The change over from Exhaust steam to Auxiliary live steam is controlled automatically by a shuttle valve operated by steam pressure from the steam chest. (See Fig. 11.)

The Exhaust Injector should not be used during shunting operations, when the engine regulator is continually being opened and closed, as this causes undue wear on the shuttle valve.

The overflow is kept shut while the injector is delivering by means of a bar pivoted at its centre, which presses down upon the overflow valve. This should be oiled as well as the water-regulator spindle.

---

78. Q.—What purpose is served by the continuous blowdown valve ?

A.—The continuous blowdown valve serves to keep down the concentration of priming and scale-forming salts in the boiler water, and it does this by allowing a small measured quantity of water to pass out of the boiler continuously whilst the regulator is open. The use of this fitting, therefore, will tend to obviate priming.

---

79. Q.—Describe how the continuous blowdown valve operates.

A.—The apparatus is fitted to the boiler back-plate having a connection from the water space above the crown of the firebox. When the regulator is open the steam taken from the steam chest to the base of the blowdown cock actuates the piston which lifts a ball valve allowing the water to discharge along a pipe leading through the tender tank to waste. (See Fig. 11A.)

When the regulator is closed the ball valve is returned to its seating by the pressure of the boiler water above.

A stop valve is interposed between the boiler and the apparatus.

Tank engines fitted with the blowdown deliver the discharge direct into the ashpan.

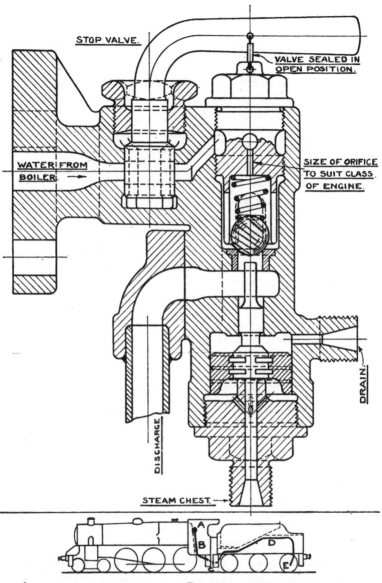

STOP VALVE.

VALVE SEALED IN OPEN POSITION.

WATER FROM BOILER.

SIZE OF ORIFICE TO SUIT CLASS OF ENGINE.

DISCHARGE

DRAIN.

STEAM CHEST.

A. BLOWDOWN VALVE.
B. COPPER DISCHARGE PIPE.
C. FLEXIBLE CONNECTION BETWEEN ENGINE & TENDER.
D. COOLING PIPE IN TENDER TANK.
E. DISCHARGE TO TRACK.

FIG. 11A.

D. D-2863.

61

80. *Q.*—Explain the principle of the firebox sand gun.

A.—A steam jet issuing from a cone situated behind the nozzle of the gun creates a partial vacuum which is used to draw sand up the supply pipe from the container situated on the fireman's side of the engine. Upon reaching the gun the sand particles are entrained by the steam jet and projected through the nozzle of the gun at high velocity towards the firebox tube plate. The nozzle of the gun is slightly offset so that when it is rotated by means of the large hand wheel situated at the rear of the mounting the jet of sand and steam is made to sweep over all parts of the tube plate in turn, and all the tubes are subjected to the scouring action of the sand blast. (See Fig. 12.)

———

81. *Q.*—How should the sand gun be operated on the road ?

A.—A place should be selected where the engine is being worked heavily in order to ensure that the steam chest pressure will be high and the blast heavy. Close the firehole doors and open the sand gun steam valve wide. Then rotate the nozzle of the gun by giving the large hand wheel at the rear of the mounting about three complete turns, afterwards closing the steam valve and restoring the firehole doors to their original position.

Whilst the gun is in operation it is advisable to lift the sand container lid and to watch the sand level inside because this will provide a check upon the proper working of the gun. If it is noticed that the sand level does not fall, it is probable that the supply pipe to the gun has become blocked and that no sand has actually reached the tubes. In this event the gun should be

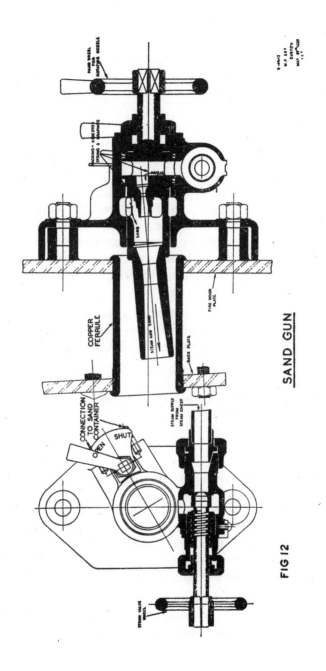

HAND WHEEL FOR ADJUSTING NOZZLE

PACKING - ASBESTOS STRING & GRAPHITE

SAND

COPPER FERRULE

STEAM AND SAND

STEAM AND SAND

FIRE DOOR PLATE

BACK PLATE

CONNECTION TO SAND CONTAINER

OPEN   SHUT

STEAM SUPPLY FROM STEAM CHEST

STEAM VALVE WHEEL

SAND GUN

FIG 12

63

reported upon arrival at destination and reliance should not be placed upon it till the stoppage has been cleared. It is also important to see that the steam valve is properly closed after use.

————

82. Q.—Explain briefly how the steam sanders work.

A.—A steam jet inside the sand ejector casting at the base of the sand pipe is employed to create a partial vacuum within the sand pipe.   A current of air is thereby induced to enter by the aperture under the hood of the sand trap at the base of the sand box, and this air passing over the surface of the sand lifts the top layer and carries it over into the sand pipe.

The sand is then caught up by the steam jet in the ejector, and forcibly blown through the sand pipe nozzle under the wheel tread.

The steam supply to the sanders is controlled by a steam valve conveniently mounted on the footplate, the control valve enables the front or back sanders to be supplied at will by the movement of a single handle.

————

83. Q.—What points do you regard as of special importance in connection with the sander gear?

A.—That the sand boxes on each side of the engine are filled and that the ends of the sand pipes are properly adjusted to deliver the sand between the tread of the wheel and the face of the rail.

Both sanders must work simultaneously for if only one side is working there is grave risk of broken coupling rods and crank pins.

84. *Q.*—Would you apply sand when the engine is slipping and the regulator is open?

A.—No, to avoid sudden strain on the motion the regulator must be closed and slipping ceased before applying sand.

———

85. *Q.*—Most modern engines are fitted with water pick-up gear; explain how this works.

A.—A movable scoop is fitted which, by the operation of a hand screw, is caused to swing downwards until its lip is a little below the level of the water in the troughs laid between the rails at certain points of the line. The forward movement of the engine then causes water to be forced up the scoop, and up a large pipe leading nearly to the top of the tender tank; the water overflows this pipe into the tank. When the water level has reached nearly to the level of the top of the pipe, the tank is full. The flow of water up the scoop is aided by a special deflector plate which banks up the water in front of the lip of the scoop. (See Fig. 13.)

———

86. *Q.*—Is particular care necessary in operating the water pick up?

A.—Yes, if the scoop is allowed to remain lowered too long the tank will overflow causing waste and also possible inconvenience to passengers seated by open windows in the coaches nearest to the engine.

The scoop must not be lowered too soon, nor ever allowed to remain lowered after passing the trough, as there is grave danger of it catching cross-over roads, wooden crossings, etc. which might cause very serious damage.

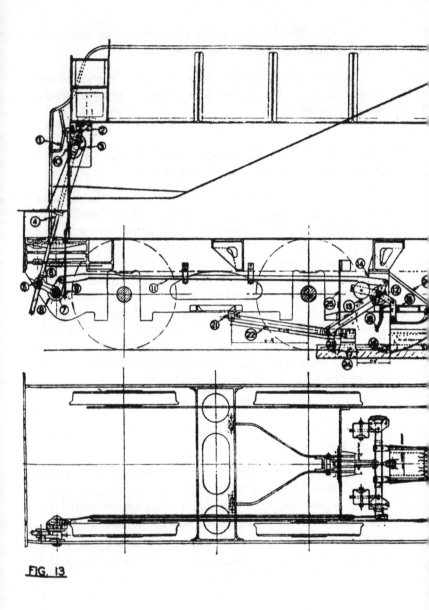

FIG. 13

66

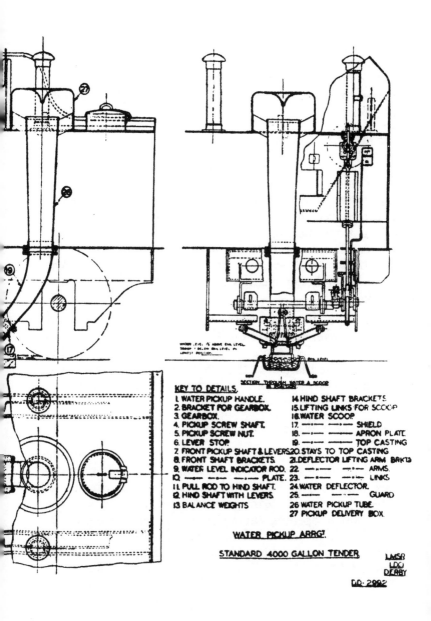

KEY TO DETAILS.

1. WATER PICKUP HANDLE.
2. BRACKET FOR GEARBOX.
3. GEARBOX.
4. PICKUP SCREW SHAFT.
5. PICKUP SCREW NUT.
6. LEVER STOP.
7. FRONT PICKUP SHAFT & LEVERS
8. FRONT SHAFT BRACKETS
9. WATER LEVEL INDICATOR ROD.
10. ————— —— PLATE.
11. PULL ROD TO HIND SHAFT.
12. HIND SHAFT WITH LEVERS.
13. BALANCE WEIGHTS

14. HIND SHAFT BRACKETS
15. LIFTING LINKS FOR SCOOP
16. WATER SCOOP
17. ——— —— SHIELD
18. ——— —— APRON PLATE
19. ——— —— TOP CASTING
20. STAYS TO TOP CASTING
21. DEFLECTOR LIFTING ARM BRKTS
22. ——— —— ARMS.
23. ——— —— LINKS.
24. WATER DEFLECTOR.
25. ——— —— GUARD
26. WATER PICKUP TUBE.
27. PICKUP DELIVERY BOX

WATER PICKUP ARRG.

STANDARD 4000 GALLON TENDER

LMSR
LDO
DERBY

D.D. 2882

67

Care should also be taken when passing over troughs with double-headed trains to see that the ash-pan, dampers, and firehole door on the train engine is closed, and the blower should also be on as a further precaution.

87. Q.—What is the smokebox?

A.—It is a chamber forming an extension at the front end of the boiler barrel. It contains the blast pipe from which the exhaust steam from the cylinders is discharged up the chimney to produce the necessary draught for the fire. Other fittings include the super-heater header when fitted, the main steam pipe or pipes, the blower and exhaust pipe from the ejectors. On some taper boiler engines the Regulator valve is in the smokebox.

In taper boiler engines baffle plates are fitted in the smokebox in front of the tubes, and below the top of the blast pipe, the purpose of these is to even up the effect of the blast over the whole tube plate, and to cut down excessive loss of fuel in the form of sparks thrown up the chimney.

88. Q.—What is a Jumper blast pipe cap?

A.—The Jumper blast pipe is an arrangement fitted to some taper boiler engines. The blast pipe cap (see Fig. 14) is fitted with a jumper ring which lifts when the exhaust steam pressure rises, thereby exposing an annular opening surrounding the normal blast pipe nozzle. The additional opening provided in this way when the jumper lifts is equal to 50 per cent. of the normal blast pipe orifice and serves to cut down the sharp blast which is usually obtained when engines are worked heavily, and the tendency to lift the fire is thereby reduced.

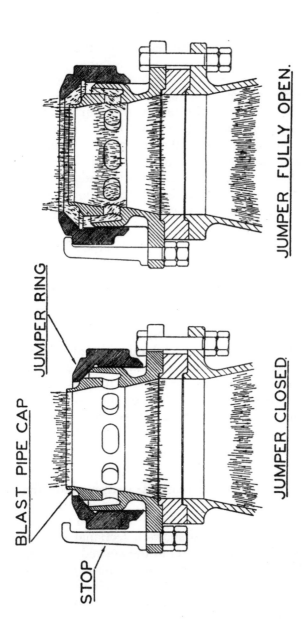

BLAST PIPE CAP

JUMPER RING

STOP

JUMPER CLOSED.

JUMPER FULLY OPEN.

JUMPER BLAST PIPE

L.M.S.R.
DRAWING OFFICE
DERBY
QQ 3209.

FIG. 14

89. *Q.*—Describe the arrangement of the Super-heater.

A.—Steam from the regulator valve is fed via the internal steampipe to the saturated steam chamber of the superheater header (see Fig. 15). From this chamber the steam is fed to the superheater elements of which there may be from 7 to 40. Each element is enclosed within a large flue tube, and extends back to within about 2 feet of the firebox tube plate, where a return bend is fitted which brings the steam back towards the smokebox.

---

90. *Q.*—What provision is made to prevent back-blast from the firebox ?

A.—Whilst working a train or light engine the Steam Blower valve *must always* be fully opened *prior* to shutting the regulator or entering a tunnel. Care should also be taken when passing over water troughs to see that the ashpan dampers and firehole on the train engine are closed and the blower on as a further precaution.

---

91. *Q.*—Describe how the carriage warming reducing valve operates.

A.—Drawing No. 16 shows a sectional view of the valve with the working parts in the normal or closed position. A general appearance of similarity to the Venturi pattern valve is apparent but this valve is slightly more simple in construction, since it employs no Venturi tube or Venturi attachment and regulation of delivery

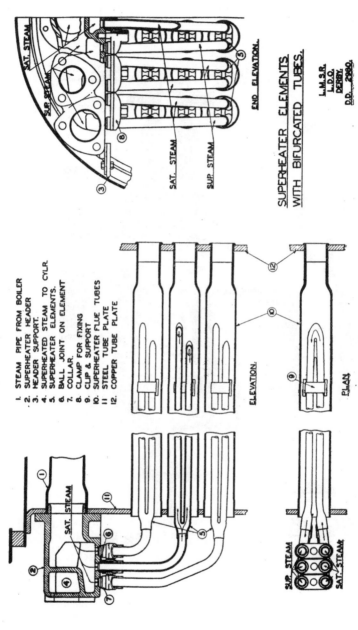

1. STEAM PIPE FROM BOILER
2. SUPERHEATER HEADER
3. HEADER SUPPORT.
4. SUPERHEATED STEAM TO CYLR.
5. SUPERHEATER ELEMENTS.
6. BALL JOINT ON ELEMENT
7. COLLAR.
8. CLAMP FOR FIXING
9. CLIP & SUPPORT
10. SUPERHEATER FLUE TUBES
11. STEEL TUBE PLATE
12. COPPER TUBE PLATE

SAT. STEAM

SUP. STEAM

END ELEVATION.

SAT. STEAM

SUP. STEAM

ELEVATION.

PLAN

SUP. STEAM

SAT. STEAM

SUPERHEATER ELEMENTS
WITH BIFURCATED TUBES.

L.M.S.R.
L.D.O.
DERBY.
D.D. 2389.

FIG. 15

71

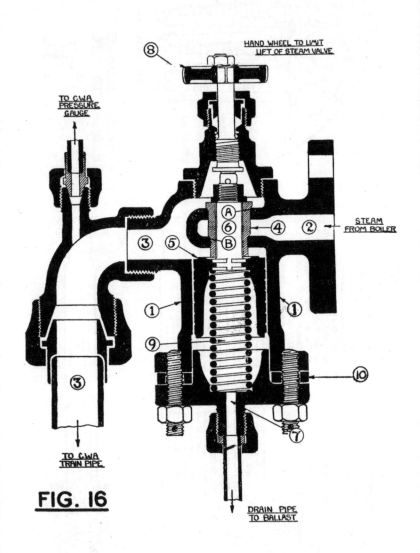

HAND WHEEL TO LIMIT
LIFT OF STEAM VALVE

TO C.WA
PRESSURE
GAUGE

STEAM
FROM BOILER

TO C.WA
TRAIN PIPE

DRAIN PIPE
TO BALLAST

FIG. 16

pressure is effected by the control piston (5) and coil spring (9) supplemented when required for use with short trains by screwing down hand wheel (8) which limits the stroke of piston (5) and the lift of the steam valve (4).

The valve body (1) is almost identical with that used for the Venturi pattern valve, having the steam inlet and delivery ports (2) and (3) arranged on each side of the upper portion and the double seated steam admission valve (4) centrally situated between them. In the lower part of the body is the cylinder housing the control piston (5) with its spring (9) in compression acting on the under side. Firmly secured to the crown of the control piston is the spindle (6) by which attachment is made to the steam valve (4). The underside of the control piston (5) is permanently open to atmosphere via the drain port (7) which allows any steam and condensate which may leak past the piston to escape freely.

When putting the valve into operation the hand wheel (8) should be unscrewed to allow ample lift on the steam valve (4) and control piston, but it may be screwed down later as required if it is found that the delivery pressure is being maintained at too high a value.

It is important to remember that although the hand wheel (8) which is fitted both to this pattern Reducing Valve and to the Venturi type will shut the valve down if screwed right down, it must not be used as a stopcock. When it is necessary to shut the valve down altogether the independent stop-plug must be used. The hand wheel is provided only for pressure regulation purposes.

In working these reducing valves, enginemen should aim at maintaining the full 50 lbs. pressure in the warming pipe on main line trains of more than ten bogie vehicles. On main line trains of ten bogie vehicles and under, 50 lbs. should be maintained for the first half hour and afterwards reduced to 30 lbs. for the remainder of the journey. Local and motor trains should only be supplied at 30 lbs. per square inch.

Let us consider the operation of the valve in the cycle of events which control the reduction of the boiler steam pressure to a steady pressure, suitable for the carriage warming system.

Steam from the boiler enters the valve by the passage (2) and flows through the top and bottom seatings (A and B) in the valve (4) into the space (3) where it exerts a pressure on the comparatively large area of the top of the piston (5). It will be seen that if no spring were provided under the piston the steam pressure acting on the top space would tend to force the piston in a downward direction, thereby closing the valve (4).

The desired carriage warming pressure is therefore controlled by the amount of lift of the valve (4) which is governed by the relationship of the downward course of the piston and the upward force of the spring (9).

Before the valves leave the works they are fitted up on the test plant and the spring adjusted to supply steam at 50 lbs. per square inch by fitting washers (10) of suitable thickness between the body casting and the bottom flange.

SECTION 6.

THE VACUUM AND STEAM BRAKES

92. *Q.*—What do you understand by the term "Automatic Vacuum brake"?

A.—A brake which under certain conditions is self acting, and which utilises the pressure of atmospheric air to operate the brake pistons.

It is misleading to say that it is a vacuum which operates the brake ; actually the brake power is applied by the pressure of the atmosphere trying to destroy a partial vacuum created on one side of the brake pistons by the ejectors on the engine.

93. *Q.*—Under what conditions would the Automatic Vacuum Brake be self acting?

A.—The brake would apply itself automatically with full power if the train became divided, so that the train pipe was broken. Similarly it would go on if any key part of the apparatus became broken or damaged so that the outside air could gain access to portions of the apparatus in which a vacuum must normally be retained in order to maintain the brake.

94. *Q.*—Name the parts of the brake apparatus in which a vacuum must be retained in order to keep the brake off

A.—The ejectors must maintain a vacuum in the train pipe and connections, in the vacuum reservoirs and on both sides of all the brake pistons throughout the train in order to keep the brake blocks off the wheels.

_____

95. Q.—What then must be done in order to apply the brake?

A.—Air must be admitted to the train pipe and its connections so that the vacuum on the lower side of every brake piston is destroyed, the vacuum in the reservoirs and upper side of the brake pistons would, however, remain. In a normal application of the brake the driver admits the desired quantity of air to the train pipe by way of the ports in the driver's disc valve, and the quantity of air he admits regulates the power of the application; full power is reached when all vacuum in the train pipe is destroyed.

_____

96. Q.—How is the train pipe vacuum measured?

A.—The train pipe vacuum is measured in " inches of mercury " and the vacuum gauges on the engine and in the brake vans are graduated in this way. A perfect vacuum corresponds to approximately 30 inches of mercury and atmospheric pressure or no vacuum to zero inches on this scale. The regulation amount of vacuum in the train pipe is 21 inches of mercury, which, it is important to bear in mind, is only a partial vacuum.

_____

97. Q.—What will be the pressure per square inch on the piston when the brake is applied if 21 inches of vacuum are shewn on the gauge?

A.—10½ lbs. per square inch. Atmospheric pressure or the weight of the air pressing upon the earth's surface is approximately 15 lbs. per square inch at sea level, and it has been found that this pressure is sufficient to support a column of mercury nearly 30 inches high. Consequently every inch of mercury in the column represents a pressure of $\frac{1}{2}$ lb. per square inch, so that 21 inches indicated in the vacuum gauge represents $10\frac{1}{2}$ lbs. pressure per square inch. Some idea of the power then available can be obtained by considering the case of a 19-inch diameter brake cylinder which is a common size. The area of the brake piston in this case will be 285 square inches and the pull produced on the brake piston rod would be $10\frac{1}{2} \times 285$ lbs. which equals 2,992 lbs. or rather more than 1 ton.

———

98.   *Q.*—How does the combination ejector create vacuum ?

   A.—A jet of steam issuing at high velocity from a cone of special shape within the ejector (see Fig. 17) draws the surrounding air forward by friction and carries it through a second and larger cone, known as the air cone, to exhaust in the smokebox.

   The removal of air in this manner from the space in the immediate vicinity of the steam jet sets up a partial vacuum inside the ejector, to fill which, air is permitted to flow past the two back stop valves from the train pipe and other portions of the brake apparatus connected to it.

   In this way it is possible to maintain the desired amount of vacuum at will in the train pipe and connections so long as the ejector is kept at work and the brake is not applied.

   The combination ejector contains two separate ejectors constructed on the above principle, each one independent of the other and possessing its

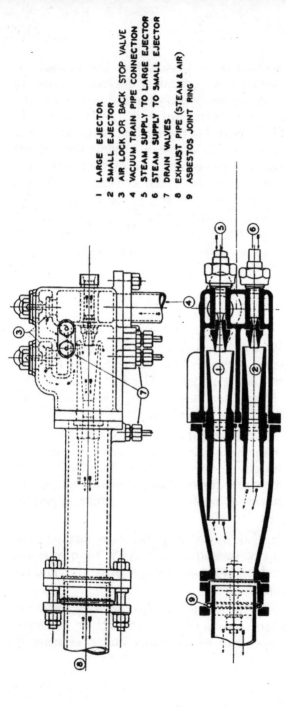

1 LARGE EJECTOR
2 SMALL EJECTOR
3 AIR LOCK OR BACK STOP VALVE
4 VACUUM TRAIN PIPE CONNECTION
5 STEAM SUPPLY TO LARGE EJECTOR
6 STEAM SUPPLY TO SMALL EJECTOR
7 DRAIN VALVES
8 EXHAUST PIPE (STEAM & AIR)
9 ASBESTOS JOINT RING

COMBINED 25 MM. & 20 MM. EJECTOR

FIG. 17

78

own set of two back stop valves. The large ejector has a steam cone usually about 25 mm. in diameter and the small ejector about 20 mm. diameter.

---

99. *Q.*—What is the object of having this combination of large and small ejectors?

A.—To avoid waste of steam. The large ejector is powerful and can create the vacuum quickly, but it uses a large quantity of steam. The small ejector is, therefore, provided for continuous use to maintain the working vacuum after the large ejector has been used to create it.

---

100. *Q.*—What purpose do the back stop valves serve in the ejector?

A.—The two back stop valves and air lock chamber are for the purpose of preventing loss of vacuum through the ejector cones when the ejector is shut down, and also to guard against steam and smokebox gases being drawn back into the train pipe and connections.

---

101. *Q.*—How is the train pipe vacuum prevented from rising above the Regulation amount of 21 inches?

A.—The vacuum relief valve is provided for the purpose. This is a spring loaded valve capable of being adjusted so that it will open and admit air to the train pipe as soon as the regulation vacuum of 21 inches is exceeded. The relief valve is generally mounted inside the cab in an accessible position because it contains a fine gauze filter to prevent entry of dust and dirt into the train pipe, and this filter requires to be cleaned and examined periodically by the Shed Staff. If this filter or air holes become choked with dirt or any other obstruction. free passage of air to the relief valve is prevented, and trouble may occur due to an excessive amount of vacuum being created in the train pipe.

---

102. Q.—What is the result of creating too high a vacuum in the train pipe?

A.—As previously explained, to release the brake the vacuum on the train pipe and reservoir sides of all the brake pistons must be equalised. If more than 21 inches is created in the reservoir of the train, any other engine having the relief valve operating at 21 inches coupled to these vehicles will be unable to equalise the brake pistons due to the excessive amount of vacuum in the reservoirs and consequently the brakes will not release properly.

---

103. Q.—If this occurs what must be done?

A.—The course to adopt in such a case is for someone to proceed down the train and pull the release cord under each vehicle. This will unseat the brake cylinder ball valves to equalise the vacuum above and below the pistons.

---

104. Q.—Describe one type of vacuum brake cylinder in common use.

A.—A pattern of vacuum brake cylinder frequently used on passenger and freight vehicles is illustrated in Fig. 18.

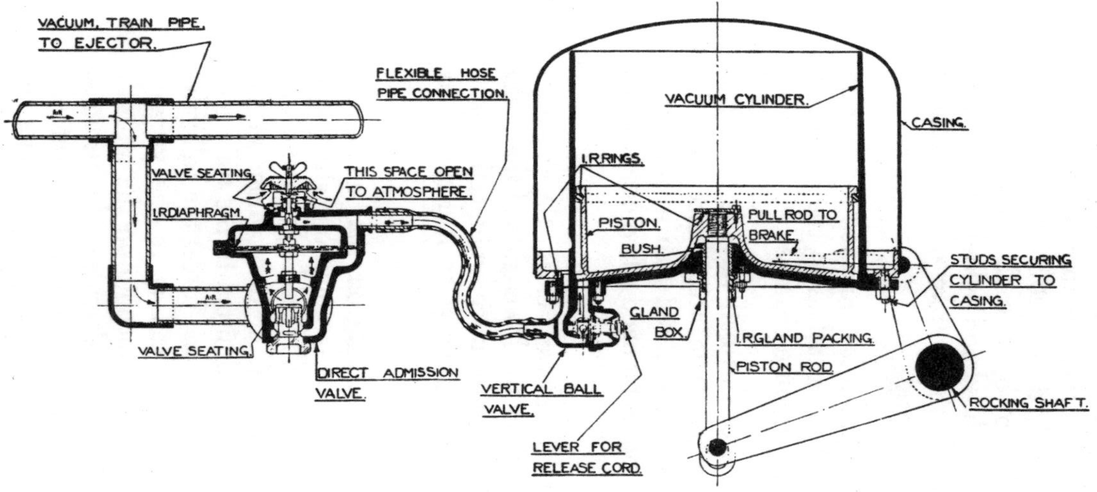

CASING.

STUDS SECURING CYLINDER TO CASING.

ROCKING SHAFT.

VACUUM CYLINDER.

PULL ROD TO BRAKE.

GLAND PACKING.

PISTON ROD.

L.R.RINGS.

PISTON.

BUSH.

GLAND BOX.

LEVER FOR RELEASE CORD.

VERTICAL BALL VALVE.

FLEXIBLE HOSE PIPE CONNECTION.

THIS SPACE OPEN TO ATMOSPHERE.

DIRECT ADMISSION VALVE.

VACUUM, TRAIN PIPE, TO EJECTOR.

VALVE SEATING.

R.DIAPHRAGM.

VALVE SEATING.

ARROWS THUS: → DENOTE DIRECTION OF AIR

DURING APPLICATION OF THE BRAKE.

FIG. 18

VACUUM BRAKE CYLINDER & D.A.VALVE WITH
CONNECTION TO TRAIN PIPE.

L.M.S.R.

DRAWING OFFICE
DERBY.
D.D. 3301. 18-5-39.

It will be seen to consist of a vacuum reservoir and cylinder combined, the cylinder proper being open at the top and enclosed within the reservoir. The brake piston is of fairly deep section and it is kept airtight within the cylinder by a rubber rolling ring nipped between the piston head and cylinder wall. The piston rod passes through the bottom of the cylinder and is kept airtight by a gland.

The brake cylinder is connected to the train pipe by a small flexible hose attached to the ball valve housing at the base of the vacuum chamber.

The purpose of this ball valve is to control movement of the brake piston in accordance with the variations in train pipe vacuum, and also to provide a means for releasing the brake by hand when necessary as described in the previous question.

This ball valve can close the vacuum chamber port, or it can place the lower side of the brake piston and the vacuum chamber in communication with each other and with the train pipe when it drops off its seating.

Running with the brake off, the ball valve is unseated, leaving the train pipe in communication with both sides of the piston, which will then be in equilibrium and resting by its own weight at the bottom of the cylinder. Immediately air is admitted to the train pipe it passes up the connecting pipe and forces the ball valve over till it seats on the port leading to the vacuum chamber, thereby retaining the vacuum on the top side of the piston. The port to the underside of the piston is, however, left open, and the air accordingly flows into the bottom of the cylinder, lifts the piston and applies the brake.

Restoration of the train pipe vacuum extracts the air from below the piston till the vacuum below equals that in the chamber above, after which the piston being equalised, will sink to the bottom of the cylinder by its own weight, allowing the brake to release. At the same time the ball valve will drop away from its seating on the vacuum chamber port, leaving the whole cylinder in its. original condition, ready for the next application.

The hand release arrangement is effected by enclosing the ball valve inside a sliding cage connected to an external lever, as shown in the drawing. When the cord is pulled, the cage is displaced, forcing the ball valve away from the vacuum chamber port, thereby placing both sides of the vacuum piston in communication with the train pipe.

———

105. *Q.*—Passenger vehicles are fitted with a communication cord which operates an alarm signal to the driver in order to stop the train in case of emergency. Describe how this arrangement operates.

A.—The communication cord consists of a chain passing through each compartment of the coach and connected at the end of the vehicle to the passengers' alarm valve, and indicating disc.

The alarm valve when operated by the chain being pulled, opens and allows air to enter the vacuum train pipe, causing a reduction in vacuum of 5 to 10 inches, which is sufficient to apply the brake with moderate force and to attract the driver's attention.

The indicating discs are normally in a horizontal position, but when the communication cord is pulled they will be turned to the vertical, thus indicating the coach from which the alarm was given.

106. Q.—Why are drip valves fitted to the vacuum pipe on the engine?

A.—One or more drip valves are always fitted to the engine train pipe to allow any moisture which may collect in the brake piping to drain away. For this reason drip valves will always be found at the lowest points on the train pipe under the engine.

The usual type is a small ball valve, which is normally held up to its seating under working conditions by atmospheric pressure acting from below. When the train pipe vacuum is totally destroyed the ball valve is unseated, thus allowing any moisture present in the train pipe to drain away.

---

107. Q.—Describe the brake action on an engine and train fitted throughout with the vacuum automatic brake.

A.—The brake is applied by the pressure of air being admitted through the ports of the driver's application valve and then passing down the train pipe from the engine.

During release the blocks on the leading vehicles will be freed first and for this reason the small ejector only should be used for release purposes whilst the train is in motion in order to avoid surging and shocks on the drawgear caused by the early release in front and continued retardation of the rear portion of the train.

---

108. Q.—How should the brake be handled then to obtain the best results?

A.—In the case of a " service application " in which full brake power is not called for, the driver should begin by destroying some 7 to 10 inches of train pipe vacuum and should hold this application till he feels the slight check which will indicate the brake has taken hold. This is known as " setting the brake." After this the brake block pressure can be varied at will by regulating the train pipe vacuum to suit requirements of the stop.

To make a full power application, the driver would put the application valve handle right over to full on position in a single movement, destroying all train pipe vacuum, and would leave it thus until speed was reduced sufficiently to permit the application to be somewhat eased.

———

3

SIGNALLING

A knowledge of signals is essential for the safe operation of trains for they indicate whether it is safe for a train to proceed, a warning that the next signal may be at danger and, at junctions, which route has been selected.

Initially signals were given by hand, but soon fixed signals were employed with indicators carried on posts. There were two basic types: disc and crossbar, and semaphore. The former had a disc and crossbar set at right angles so that when turned, only one was displayed, the other being at right angles to an oncoming train. A disc indicated 'Line Clear' while a crossbar indicated 'Stop'.

The first semaphore signal arms were mounted in a pivot in a slot in the post and could show three positions: horizontal indicated 'Stop', lowered to 45 degrees indicated 'Caution' and when hidden inside the slot, 'Clear'.

Slotted signals proved dangerous and were abolished after a terrible accident of 21 February 1876. That evening a severe blizzard swept across eastern and central England. At Holme, south of Peterborough, the Great Northern Railway signalman had been instructed to shunt an Up coal train into a siding to allow the Up Flying Scotsman to overtake. Although he had set his signals at 'Danger', the goods train ran past without stopping.

The next two boxes were not in telegraphic communication with him, so he telegraphed to Abbots Ripton instructing the signalman there to shunt the goods.

When the mineral train arrived at Abbots Ripton the driver saw a red lamp waved from the box and drew to a halt. The signalman called out, 'Siding! Shove them back, the Scotsman's standing at Wood Walton.'

But just about that moment, the signalman at Wood Walton was horrified to see the Scotsman fly past his signals at Danger. When the

Scotsman reached Abbots Ripton the last six wagons of the coal train were still on the main line. The express engine struck them, overturned and the coaches piled against it, blocking both lines. The Abbots Ripton signalman unsuccessfully tried to warn Huntingdon of the accident and to stop all Down trains.

Driver Bray on the engine of the coal train was unharmed and ordered his fireman to go forward with detonators to protect the Down line and sent a clerk to the signal box for permission for him to take his engine forward to warn oncoming Down trains. Permission granted, he set off with his guard on the right of the footplate waving a red lamp.

A foreman platelayer was also protecting the Down line and already had placed detonators by the Abbots Ripton Down distant signal 1,100 yards from the accident when an express passed him at over 50 mph.

The express driver, hearing the detonators, immediately closed the regulator, reversed and whistled for the two guards to apply the brakes – continuous brakes worked from the engine not being fitted. As soon as he had done this, he caught a glimpse of a red lamp being waved and heard the goods engine whistling.

The rails were slippery with ice and snow, so the Down express was still moving at 15 to 20 mph when it struck the derailed Scotsman. Fourteen people were killed, most losing their lives in the second collision.

On investigation it was found that snow, driven by the gale and then frozen, had wedged the signal arms in the slot so that the balance weights could not return them to 'Danger'. Furthermore, the signal wires were covered with 3 inches of ice and Joshua Pallinder, a signal fitter, informed the subsequent inquiry that he had to hack ice off the Abbots Ripton signals to release the arms from the slotted posts and tie a 36 lb rail chair to the balance weight of the Up distant signal before it would return to 'Danger'. Even when he had freed the arm of the Down distant at Wood Walton, it automatically dropped back to 'Clear' due to the weight of the snow on the signal wire.

In the early days of railways, stations were not linked by telegraph so there was no way of determining whether a train departing from one station had actually reached the next. Trains were roughly kept apart by the time interval system, a signal being kept at 'Danger' for three minutes after the passing of a train, followed by seven minutes at 'Caution' before being set at 'Clear'. The drawback with this method was that a train may have broken down out of sight of a despatching station and if so, there was no means of warning a following train that the line was blocked.

With the introduction of the telegraph, trains could be kept apart by distance. The line was divided into sections and a train not permitted to enter a section until it had been cleared by the previous train. Safety was further improved by interlocking of points and signals whereby, either mechanically or electrically, it was impossible for a signalman to set up a conflicting route.

Particularly in fog, or falling snow, it was difficult for a driver to stop in time when seeing an adverse signal. To overcome this problem, distant signals were provided to give advance warning of the position of a home signal. Initially the distant signals were indistinguishable from home signals, but a fish-tail notch was introduced in 1872 on those belonging to the London, Brighton & South Coast Railway and became universal after 1877. In the early twentieth century distant signal arms were further distinguished by being painted yellow and displaying a yellow light.

In the 1920s the LMS, LNER and SR standardised on the upper quadrant arm, as with this pattern light, pressed-steel construction could be used, merely the weight of the arm returning it to danger if a wire broke, whereas a lower quadrant signal required a heavy spectacle to perform this task.

On underground railways the electric colour light signal appeared. There were two types: the searchlight with one lamp and lens, a colour filter being moved in front to show different aspects; and the multiple-lamp type, featuring separate lamps and coloured lenses for each aspect. Colour light signalling permitted a fourth aspect to be shown, a double yellow indicating that the next but one signal was at 'Danger'. This allows a driver to regulate his speed better to the circumstances and may avoid him having to come to a dead stop.

FIXED SIGNALS.

34. Fixed signals consist of distant, stop and subsidiary signals.

In certain instances signals are repeated, in which cases the additional signals are known as repeating signals.

Automatic signals are signals controlled by the passage of trains.

Semi-automatic signals are signals which are controlled by the passage of trains and in addition can be controlled from a signal box or ground frame.

35. (a) Semaphore signals are generally of the two-position type, the indications being shown thus :—

DISTANT SIGNALS.

By Day.   By Night.

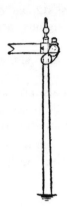

Caution position.   Yellow (or
                           red where
                           used) light.

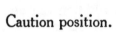

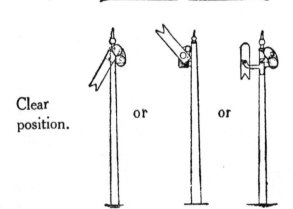

Clear   or   or   Green
position.   light.

STOP SIGNALS (HOME, STARTING AND ADVANCED STARTING).

By Day.   By Night

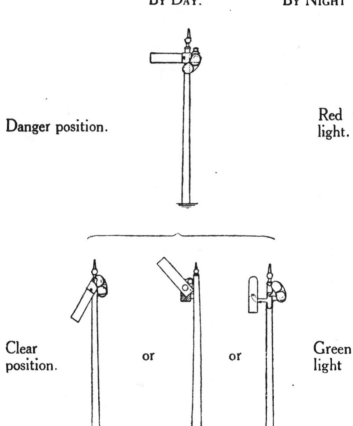

Danger position.

Red light.

Clear position.   or   or   Green light

(*b*) Other types of signals include :—

(i.) Three-position semaphore signals—the indications being shown thus :—

By Day.   By Night.

Danger position.   Red light.

Caution position.   Yellow light.

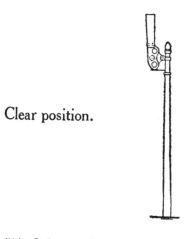

Clear position.

Green
light.

(ii.) Colour light signals—not provided with semaphore arms, the day and night indications being given by means of lights only, i.e., red for Danger, yellow for Caution, and green for Clear.

In some cases colour light signals will exhibit two yellow lights. This indication means—Pass next signal at restricted speed, and if applicable to a junction may denote that the points are set for a diverging route over which the speed restriction shown in the Appendix applies.

(iii.) Repeating signals of the banner type consisting of a black arm in a circular frame, illuminated at night.

(iv.) Subsidiary signals in the form of disc signals, or of the banner type with red or yellow arm in a circular frame, or position light signals, or semaphore signals with small arms—the normal indications being :—

By Day.	By Night.
Red disc.	Red light or white light.
Yellow disc.	Yellow light.
Red arm in horizontal position in a circular frame or on a white disc.	Red light, white light or the day normal indication being illuminated.
Yellow arm in horizontal position in a circular frame or on a white disc.	Yellow light or the day normal indication being illuminated.
Position light signals with two white lights or one red or yellow light on the left and one white light on the right in horizontal position, or no lights.	Same as by day.
Small red semaphore arm, or small white semaphore arm with red stripes, in the horizontal position.	Red light, white light, or no light.
Small yellow semaphore arm in the horizontal position.	Yellow light.

The Proceed indication by day is given by the disc being turned off or the arm lowered or raised or in the case of position light signals by two white lights at an angle of 45 degrees ; and by night by a green light or the day Proceed indication being illuminated or in the case of position light signals by two white lights at an angle of 45 degrees.

In some cases the signals are distinguished thus :—

Calling-on   by the letter **C.**
Warning   ,, ,,   ,, **W.**
Shunt-ahead ,, ,,   ,, **S.**

Ground signals (colour light)—the normal indication

being a yellow or red light and the Proceed indication a green light.

(c) Automatic stop signals are identified by a white plate with a horizontal black band.

Semi-automatic stop signals are identified by a white plate bearing the word " SEMI " above a horizontal black band.

(d) Back lights, where provided for fixed signals, show a white light to the Signalman when the signals are at Danger, and are obscured when the signals are in the Clear position. In the case of position light signals where back lights are provided, they are also exhibited in some cases when the signals are at Clear.

(e) Fixed signals, as a rule, are so placed as to indicate by their positions the lines to which they apply. Where more than one stop or subsidiary signal is fixed on the same side of a post the top signal applies to the line on the extreme left, and the second signal to the line next in order from the left and so on.

At some diverging points, only one semaphore arm or colour light signal is provided together with an indicator exhibiting a letter or number showing the line over which the train will run,

or

only one colour light signal is provided together with a junction indicator exhibiting a line of white light or lights by day and by night when a Proceed aspect is given for a diverging route (see diagram below) ; for movements along the straight route no junction indication will be exhibited.

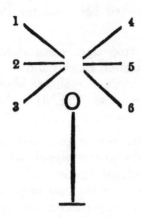

Indication 1 is the equivalent of signal 1 when " Off "

    ,,   2   ,,   ,,   ,,   2   ,,   ,,

    ,,   3   ,,   ,,   ,,   3   ,,   ,,

(See diagrams below)

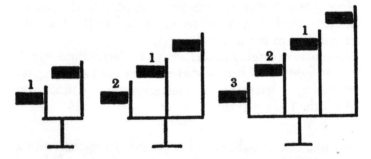

Indications 4, 5 and 6 relate to routes on the right hand of the straight line and apply in a similar manner.

(f) Except in the case of automatic signals or where otherwise authorised, the normal position of fixed signals is Danger, or Caution in the case of distant signals.

NOTE.—*Additions to this Rule are contained in separate publications issued by the Companies concerned.*

DISTANT SIGNALS.

36. (a) Distant signals are placed at some distance in rear of the home signals to which they apply, and where necessary below the home, starting or advanced starting signal, applicable to the same line, of the signal box in rear.

(b) Where only one distant signal is provided for a diverging junction such signal applies to all trains approaching it.

(c) The Caution position of a distant signal indicates to a Driver that he must be prepared to stop at the home signal to which it applies.

STOP SIGNALS

(*HOME, STARTING AND ADVANCED STARTING*).

37. (a) Where starting signals are provided the home signal must not be passed at Danger except as follow :—

EXCEPTIONS.

(i.) *When subsidiary signals are lowered (Rules 45 and 47).*

(ii.) *When a train is required to enter an obstructed line for the purpose of rendering assistance and the driver is so authorised by the signalman.*

(iii.) *When signal is defective or cannot be lowered owing to failure of apparatus or during repairs (Rules 77, 78, and 81).*

(iv.) *When single line working is in operation during repairs or obstruction (Rule 197).*

(v.) **When necessary for an engine to be brought to the rear of a train to attach or detach vehicles or to remove vehicles from the line (Rule 116 (b)).**

Where a home signal controls the entrance of trains into the section ahead the provisions of Rule 38 apply to such signal.

(b) Where a starting signal is not provided and it is necessary for a train which has been stopped at the home signal to be brought within that signal before the line ahead is clear, the Signalman before lowering the home signal must verbally inform the Driver as to the state of the line ahead and what is required of him.

If, when the train is stopped at the home signal, it is not possible for the verbal communication to be made, Rule 40 must be observed.

When the line ahead is clear, the signal for the train to proceed must be given by the Signalman showing the Driver a green hand signal held steadily.

38 (a) Where advanced starting signals are provided, the starting signal must not be passed at Danger except as follow :—

EXCEPTIONS.

(i.) *When subsidiary signals are lowered (Rules 45 and 47).*

(ii.) *When a train is required to enter an obstructed line for the purpose of rendering assistance and the driver is so authorised by the signalman.*

(iii.) *When signal is defective, or cannot be lowered owing to failure of apparatus or during repairs (Rules 77, 78 and 81).*

(iv.) *When single line working is in operation during repairs or obstruction (Rule 197).*

(*b*) Home signals where starting signals are not provided, starting signals where advanced starting signals are not provided, and advanced starting signals, control the entrance of trains into the section ahead, and must not be passed at Danger except as follow :—

EXCEPTIONS.

(i.) *When calling-on, warning or shunt-ahead signals are lowered.   (Rules 44, 45 and 46.)*

(ii.) *Where the position of siding connections or crossover roads renders it necessary for the signal controlling the entrance to the section ahead to be passed for shunting purposes and a shunt-ahead signal is not provided, a Driver may, for this purpose pass the signal at Danger upon being directed to do so by the Signalman, either verbally or by a green hand signal held steadily, but he must not go forward on his journey until the signal controlling the entrance to the section ahead has been lowered.*

(iii.) *During the failure of instruments or bells when it is necessary for a train to be brought within the protection of the home signal, in accordance with Block Regulation 25, clause* (**e**), *and a shunt-ahead signal is not provided, upon the Driver being* instructed verbally by the Signalman, but the Driver must not proceed on his journey until the starting (or advanced starting) signal has been lowered, or until authorised to do so in accordance with clause (b) of Rule 37.

(iv.) (Deleted.)

(v.) When signal is defective, or cannot be lowered owing to failure of apparatus or during repairs. (Rules 77, 78 and 81).

(vi.) When single line working is in operation during repairs or obstruction. (Rule 197.)

(vii.) When a train is required to enter an obstructed section and the Driver is instructed verbally by the Signalman. (Block Regulation 14.)

(viii.) When an engine (or train) is required to enter a section to examine the line, and the Driver is instructed verbally by the Signalman. (Block Regulation 14A.)

(ix.) When necessary to allow the front portion of a divided train to proceed into the section ahead. (Rule 182.)

(x.) When necessary for a train to follow first portion of a divided train. (Block Regulation 20.)

(xi.) When necessary for a train to travel through section after runaway train or vehicles are removed from the section. (Block Regulations 22 and 23.)

(xii.) **When necessary at stations where Absolute Block Working is in force for an engine to be brought to the rear of a train to attach or detach vehicles or to remove vehicles from the section (Rule 116 (b)).**

39. (*a*) When a stop signal is at Danger the stop signal next in rear of it worked from the same signal box must not be lowered for an approaching train until the train is close to such signal and has been brought quite, or nearly, to a stand.

During fog or falling snow, the Driver of a train stopped, or nearly stopped, at a signal next in rear of a starting signal must, when practicable, be verbally informed that he is only to draw forward towards the starting signal.

NOTE.—*This clause (a) does not apply to multiple-aspect signals.*

(*b*) **During fog or falling snow, except where track circuit or other apparatus is provided to avoid the necessity for trainmen having to go to the signal box to carry out Rule 55, a train must not be allowed to proceed to an advanced starting signal, starting signal or home signal situated ahead of the signal box to await acceptance from the signal box in advance, unless the Signalman is satisfied the signal concerned is at Danger, and that the rear part of a train when standing at that signal will be within his view.**

(*c*) The Driver of any train which has been stopped or brought nearly to a stand in accordance with clause (*a*), must, after the signal has been lowered, draw slowly forward to the next signal and be prepared to stop at the signal box if necessary. When proceeding towards a starting or advanced starting signal at Danger, he must (except for station duties or shunting purposes, or as shown below) only proceed as far as is necessary to leave the last vehicle well clear of junction points and junction crossings, and, as far as practicable, within sight of the Signalman. Where there are no junction points or junction crossings the Driver must bring his train to a stand in a convenient position for the carrying out of Rule 55.

Where track circuit or other apparatus is provided in connection with the starting or advanced starting signal, to avoid the necessity for trainmen having to go to the signal box to carry out Rule 55, the Driver must draw forward to the starting or advanced starting signal.

40. When a Signalman wishes to communicate verbally with a Driver he must stop the train at the signal next in rear of the signal box for this purpose, but if it is not then possible for the verbal communication to be made, he must lower the signal (or subsidiary signal where provided) for the train to draw forward, and stop it at the signal box by exhibiting a red hand signal. The Driver must not proceed until he clearly understands the verbal communication and has received the necessary authority.

41. (a) When a train is allowed to go forward under Block Regulation 5 and a stop signal is provided in advance of the box, the Signalman must, if the train has not already passed the home signal, bring it quite or nearly to a stand at that signal before lowering it, and, unless a fixed warning signal or warning indication is provided, must as the train is approaching the box exhibit to the Driver a green hand signal, held steadily, which the Driver must acknowledge by giving

a short whistle as an indication that he understands that the section is clear to the next home signal, but that the station or junction ahead is blocked. The necessary fixed signals may then be lowered for the train to proceed. If the Driver does not acknowledge the hand signal the signal controlling the entrance to the section ahead must not be lowered until the train has been brought to a stand at it.

If there is not a stop signal in advance of the box, the Signalman must, unless a fixed warning signal or warning indication is provided, stop the train in accordance with Rule 40, and verbally instruct the Driver that the section is clear to the next home signal but that the station or junction ahead is blocked, after which a green hand signal, held steadily, must be exhibited to the Driver.

If the train is assisted by an engine in rear, or two trains are coupled together, a green hand signal, held steadily, must be exhibited to the Driver of each engine.

Where a warning signal or warning indication is provided the green hand signal must not be exhibited.

(b) Except where instructions are issued to the contrary, when a train has passed the signal box and is brought to a stand owing to the signal controlling the entrance to the section ahead being at Danger, the lowering of such signal must be taken by the Driver as an indication that the section is clear to the next home signal but that the station or junction ahead is blocked, and he must regulate the speed of his train accordingly.

REPEATING SIGNALS.

42. Repeating signals, where provided, are placed in the rear of, and repeat the indication given by, the signals to which they apply.

When a repeating signal indicates that the stop signal is at Danger, the Driver must proceed cautiously towards the stop signal.

MULTIPLE-ASPECT SIGNALS.

43. Where three-aspect signals are provided, the Caution aspect indicates to a Driver that he must be prepared to stop at the next signal, and the Clear aspect indicates that he must be prepared to find the next signal showing either the Caution or Clear aspect.

Where colour light signals having more than three aspects are provided, one yellow light indicates to a Driver that he must be prepared to stop at the next signal, and two yellow lights indicate that he must be prepared to **pass the next signal at restricted speed, and if applicable to a junction may denote that the points are set for a diverging route over which the speed restriction shown in the Appendix applies.**

SUBSIDIARY SIGNALS.
Calling-on Signals.

44. (*a*) Calling-on signals, where provided, are placed below the signal controlling the entrance to the section ahead, and when lowered authorise the Driver to proceed

forward cautiously into the section ahead as far as the line is clear.

The lowering of the calling-on signal does not authorise the next stop signal to be passed at Danger.

(*b*) Except where authorised, the calling-on signal must not be lowered until the train has been brought to a stand at it.

WARNING SIGNALS.

45. (*a*) Warning signals, where provided, are placed below stop signals, and when the warning signal is lowered the Driver must understand that the line is clear only as far as the next stop signal. The lowering of a warning signal fixed under the signal controlling the entrance to the section ahead must be taken as an indication that the section is clear to the next home signal but that the station or junction ahead is blocked, and the Driver must regulate the speed of his train accordingly.

(*b*) The warning signal must not be lowered until the train has been brought quite, or nearly, to a stand at it.

SHUNT-AHEAD SIGNALS.

46. Shunt-ahead signals, where provided, are placed below the signal controlling the entrance to the section ahead, and when lowered, authorise the latter signal to be passed at Danger for shunting purposes only, and a train must not proceed on its journey until the signal controlling the entrance to the section has been lowered.

DRAW-AHEAD AND SHUNTING SIGNALS.

47. Draw-ahead signals, where provided, are placed below stop signals not controlling the entrance to the section ahead.

Shunting signals are used to regulate the passage of trains from a siding to a running line, from a running line to a siding, between one running line and another, and to control shunting operations.

Draw-ahead and shunting signals apply when lowered as far as the line is clear towards the next signal only, but the lowering or turning off of such signals does not authorise the next signal to be passed at Danger.

Except as provided for in Rules 40 and 96, the draw-ahead signal may be lowered after the train has been brought quite or nearly to a stand at it.

Shunting signals of the types described below may be passed, without being turned off or lowered, for movements in a direction for which the signal when turned off or lowered does not apply :—

Signal having a yellow arm or disc.

,,   ,,   yellow arm on a white disc.

,,   ,,   yellow light.

Position light signal having yellow and white lights.

SIGNAL CONTROLLING EXIT FROM SIDING.

48. (a) Where a signal is provided to control the exit from a siding and a train is ready to depart, a Driver must not proceed until such signal has been lowered, nor must a Driver whilst waiting for the signal to be lowered, allow his engine to stand foul of any other line

(*b*) When a signal applies to more than one siding and more than one engine is in the sidings, a Driver must not move towards the signal so as to foul any other siding until he has been instructed to do so by the person in charge of the shunting operations.

TRAINS SHUNTING OR RUNNING IN WRONG DIRECTION.

49. Distant, home, starting, advanced starting, and subsidiary signals placed under stop signals, apply only to trains travelling in the proper direction on the running lines, and must not be used for any other purpose, except as provided in Rule 197. Trains moving in the wrong direction on any running line or shunting from one running line to another, or shunting into, or out of, sidings connected with running lines must, unless fixed signals are provided for such movements, be signalled verbally, or by hand signal, as occasion may require.

HAND SIGNALS.

50. (*a*) (Deleted.)

(*b*) A red hand signal indicates Danger and, except as shown below, must be used only when it is necessary to stop a train. In the absence of a red light, any light waved violently denotes Danger.

EXCEPTIONS.

1. *To indicate to Driver and Guard during fog or falling snow that a distant signal in which a red light is used is at Caution. Rules 59, 91 and 194.*

   Red hand signal held steadily by Fogsignalman.

2. *To indicate to Driver that a distant signal in which a red light is used is defective and cannot be placed at Caution. Rule 81.*

   Red hand signal held steadily by Handsignalman at distant signal.

3. *To indicate to Driver that single line working is in operation. Rule 200.*

   Red hand signal held steadily by Handsignalman at a distant signal in which a red light is used, applicable to the line upon which single line working is in operation.

(c) A yellow hand signal indicates Caution and is used for the following purposes :—

1. To indicate to Driver and Guard during fog or falling snow that a distant signal in which a yellow light is used is at Caution.—Rules 59, 91 and 194.

   Yellow hand signal held steadily by Fogsignalman.

2. To indicate to Driver that a distant signal in which a yellow light is used is defective and cannot be placed at Caution.—Rule 81.

Yellow hand signal held steadily by Handsignalman at distant signal.

3. To indicate to Driver that single line working is in operation.—Rule 200.

Yellow hand signal held steadily by Handsignalman at a distant signal, in which a yellow light is used, applicable to the line upon which single line working is in operation.

4. To authorise Driver to pass a multiple-aspect signal which is disconnected or out of order.—Rule 78.

Yellow hand signal held steadily by Handsignalman at the signal.

5. To indicate to Driver and Guard during fog or falling snow that a multiple-aspect signal is at Caution.—Rule 91.

Yellow hand signal held steadily by Fogsignalman.

(d) The purposes for which a white hand signal is used are as follow :—

1. Move away from hand signal, in shunting.—Rule 52.

White light waved slowly up and down.

2. Move towards hand signal, in shunting.—Rule 52.

White light waved slowly from side to side across body.

3. To indicate to Guard of passenger train that all is right for the train to proceed.—Rule 141.

White light held steadily above the head by person in charge.

4. To acknowledge Guard's green hand signal.—Rule 142, clause (d).

White light held steadily by Fireman.

5. To indicate to Signalman that points require to be turned.—Rule 69.

White light moved quickly above the head by Guard or Shunter.

NOTE.—The above paragraph 5 does not apply on the Great Western Railway

6. To indicate to Guard that Driver of train is carrying train staff. (Regulations for working on single lines by train staff and ticket.)	**White hand signal held steadily by Signalman.**

(e) The purposes for which a green hand signal is used are as follow :—

1. Move slowly away from hand signal, in shunting.—Rule 52.	Green light waved slowly up and down.
2. Move slowly towards hand signal, in shunting.—Rule 52.	Green light waved slowly from side to side across body.
3. Guard's signal to Driver to start, and to indicate that Guard or Shunter has re-joined train.—Rules 55, 141 and 142.	Green light held steadily above the head, or green flag (where used) waved above the head.
4. To indicate by night to Fireman of goods train after starting that his train is complete.—Rule 142.	Green light waved slowly from side to side by Guard from his van.
5. To indicate to Driver that train is divided.—Rule 182.	Green hand signal waved slowly from side to side by Signalman.
6. To give an All Right signal to Driver where there is no starting signal.—Rules 37 and 38.	Green hand signal held steadily by Signalman.
7. To authorise Driver to move after having been stopped at signal box.—Rule 54.	Green hand signal held steadily by Signalman.
8. To authorise Driver to pass signal controlling entrance to the section ahead at Danger, for shunting purposes.—Rule 38.	Green hand signal held steadily by Signalman.

9. To indicate to Driver and Guard during fog or falling snow that the signal is at Clear.—Rules 91 and 127 (xxii.).

Green hand signal held steadily by Fogsignalman.

10. To reduce speed for permanent-way operations.—Rules 60, 127 (xxi.), 217 and 218.

Green hand signal waved slowly from side to side by Handsignalman.

11. To give an All Right signal to Driver when fixed signal (other than a multiple-aspect signal) is disconnected or out of order.—Rules 78 and 81.

Green hand signal held steadily by Handsignalman at the signal.

12. To authorise Driver to draw forward to signal box when fixed signal is out of order, before Handsignalman has arrived.—Rule 81.

Green hand signal held steadily by Signalman at the box.

13. To indicate to Driver that section is clear, but station or junction is blocked.—Rule 41.

Green hand signal held steadily by Signalman as train is approaching the box or after giving verbal warning.

14. To indicate to Driver of goods train, timed to stop at a station, that there is nothing to pick up, and that if there is nothing to put off the train it need not stop.—Rule 144.

Green hand signal waved slowly up and down.

15. To indicate that catch points, spring points, or unworked trailing points are in right position for train to pass in facing direction.—Rule 196.

Green hand signal held steadily by Handsignalman at points.

16. To caution Driver entering terminal station, or station worked under special instructions, if line is not clear. —Rule 96.

Green hand signal held steadily by Signalman after bringing train to a stand.

17. To caution Driver of following train.—(Regulations for working on goods lines where the Absolute Block System is not in operation or where no special Regulations are in force.)

Green hand signal held steadily by Signalman after bringing train to a stand.

18. **To authorise Driver to pass fixed signal at Danger when attaching, detaching or removing vehicles.— Rule 116(b).**

Green hand signal held steadily by Signalman.

19. **To indicate to Guard that Driver of train is carrying ticket. (Regulations for working on single lines by train staff and ticket).**

Green hand signal held steadily by Signalman.

51. In the absence of flags :—

(a) Both arms raised above the head denotes Danger or stop, thus :—

(NOTE.—*When riding on or in a vehicle either arm moved up and down denotes stop.*)

(*b*) Either arm held in a horizontal position and the hand moved up and down denotes Caution or slow down, thus :—

(*c*) Either arm held above the head denotes All Right, thus :—

(*d*) Either arm moved in a circular manner away from the body denotes move away from hand signal, thus :—

(e) Either arm moved across and towards the body at shoulder level denotes move towards hand signal, thus :—

52. In shunting operations by night, or when necessary during fog or falling snow, a white light waved slowly up and down means move away from the person giving the signal ; a white light waved slowly from side to side across the body means move towards the person giving the signal.

A green light used instead of a white light, indicates that these shunting movements are to be made slowly.

53. (a) Hand lamps and flags, when used as signals, except where they are employed for the purpose of indicating the point of an obstruction, must be held ; they must not be placed upon, or fixed in, the ground or elsewhere.

(b) When a Signalman gives a hand signal, it must in all cases be exhibited outside the signal box.

54. After a train has been brought to a stand by a hand Danger signal from a signal box, the Driver must not move, although the hand Danger signal may have been withdrawn, until a green hand signal has been

exhibited by the Signalman. This All Right hand signal will not authorise the Driver to pass a fixed signal at Danger unless he has been verbally instructed by the Signalman to do so.

4

ACTION TO BE TAKEN IF A TRAIN IS HELD ON A RUNNING LINE

When a railway accident occurred, the Board of Trade investigated and sometimes a new rule was introduced to prevent a reoccurrence.

Early on 11 November 1890 a Down goods was shunted to the Up line at Norton Fitzwarren, west of Taunton, to allow a fast goods to overtake. Unfortunately the signalman completely forgot about the goods train shunted to the Up line and accepted a fast Up boat train from Plymouth.

With only two eight-wheel coaches and a van, this hurtled into the station at 60 mph and crashed into the goods train. Despite the speed of the impact, the broad gauge locomotive and train remained upright and in line, although the standard gauge goods train debris made a pile 30 feet high. Unfortunately ten of the fifty passengers were killed and nine seriously injured. To prevent a repetition, Rule 55 was introduced and adopted by all railways in Great Britain

It ordered that when a train halted at a signal, the driver was to blow his whistle and if the signalman did not lower his board, after three minutes in clear weather, or immediately in fog or falling snow, then the driver must send a fireman, guard, or shunter to the signal box to inform the signalman of the train's presence and not leave until a collar had been placed over the relevant signal lever to prevent a conflicting movement being made. Additionally, the person sent was to sign the train register.

DETENTION OF TRAINS ON RUNNING LINES.

55. (a) (i.) When a train has been brought to a stand owing to a stop signal being at Danger, the Driver must sound the engine whistle, and, **if the signal is not immediately lowered, the Guard, Shunter or Fireman must (except as shown in paragraphs (ii.) and (iii.) of this clause), at once go to the signal box** and remind the Signalman of the position of the train, and, except as provided in clause (*f*), remain in the box until permission is obtained for the train to proceed.

(ii.) **When a train has been brought to a stand owing to a stop signal being at Danger and the signal bears a sign as shown in diagram No. 1 it will not be necessary for the Guard, Shunter or Fireman to go to the signal box to remind the Signalman of the position of the train. If the signal bears a sign as shown in diagram No. 2 the Fireman, or, in cases where vehicles are in front of the engine, the Guard or Shunter, must at once press the plunger fixed on the signal post or on a pillar near by.**

Except where the indication " RULE 55

EXEMPT—PRESS KEY " is given, the sound-ing of the bell at the signal post or pillar in response to the plunger being pressed is an indication that the signal so given has been effective and it will not be necessary for the Fireman, Guard or Shunter to go to the signal box to remind the Signalman of the position of the train, but, if the bell does not sound, the instructions respecting the Fire-man, Guard or Shunter going to the signal box to remind the Signalman of the position of the train must be carried out. Where the indication " RULE 55 EXEMPT—PRESS KEY " is given at the signal post or the pillar, the plunger must be operated at once and this will indicate in the signal box the position of the train without a bell sounding at the signal post or pillar. In such cases it will not be necessary for the Fireman, Guard or Shunter to go to the signal box to remind the Signalman of the position of the train after the plunger has been pressed.

Diagram No. 1.   Diagram No. 2.

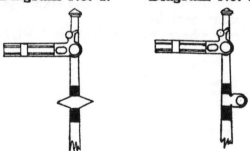

In some cases the signs shown in diagrams No. 1 and No. 2 are illuminated or the actual position of the fireman's call box is indicated by a lamp which is illuminated during darkness.

In cases where a train has been brought to a stand at a stop signal and the man responsible for carrying out this Rule has operated the plunger of the instrument provided, and the Signalman then lowers the signal for the engine or engine and part of the train to draw forward for shunting operations or any other cause leaving part of the train on the running line, the plunger must again be operated by the person responsible for the rear part of the train when the engine or engine and part of the train has passed the stop signal and it has been placed to Danger.

The appliances and indicators referred to in this paragraph (ii.) must not be taken as applying to a train or vehicle which has been shunted on to the opposite running line, or has come to a stand after making any movement other than proceeding along the right running line in its ordinary course ; in such circumstances, the man responsible for carrying out this Rule must in all cases proceed immediately to the signal box as laid down in clause (b).

(iii.) In the case of single lines, if the Driver is in possession of the train staff or electric token, it will not be necessary for the man to go to the signal box to remind the Signalman of the position of the train in connection with trains detained at home signals.

(*b*) When a train or vehicle has passed a stop signal for the purpose of being crossed to another line, or to be let into a siding, or has been shunted on to the opposite running line, or placed on either a main or branch line at a junction, or when a train or vehicle has been shunted from a siding on to a running line for the purpose of being crossed to another line, the Guard, Shunter or Fireman must (except where printed instructions are given to the contrary), when the train or vehicle comes to a stand, and is detained, *proceed immediately* to the signal box and remind the Signalman of the position of the train or vehicle, and, except as provided in clause (*f*), remain in the box until the Signalman can give permission for it to proceed or to be shunted clear of the running lines.

(*c*) The duty of going to the signal box must (except in the case of rail motors, motor trains and electric trains) be performed by the Guard, Shunter, or Fireman who is nearest to the signal box.

Except where instructions are issued to the contrary, in the case of rail motors, motor trains and electric trains, the duty of going to the signal box to remind the Signalman of the position of the train or of operating the appliances referred to in paragraph (ii.) of clause (*a*) must be performed by the Guard or Shunter ; when there is no Guard or Shunter with a rail motor or motor

train the duty must be performed by the Fireman if both men are on the engine and by the Driver if he is in the opposite end of the train to the engine, and, where bells are provided, before leaving the compartment he must give the special bell code (6 beats) to the Fireman.

(*d*) When a train or vehicle has been shunted from one running line to another, the Guard, Shunter, or Fireman, as the case may be, must, before going to the signal box, satisfy himself that the line from which the train or vehicle has been shunted is clear.

(*e*) Sufficient time must be allowed for the Guard, Shunter or Fireman to rejoin the train before the signal is lowered, and the Driver must not, when the signal is lowered, go forward until he has received a hand signal from the Guard or Shunter to intimate that he has rejoined the train. By day the hand signal must be given by holding one arm above the head or the waving of a green flag above the head, and by night a green light held steadily above the head.

Except as shown below, if the signal box is ahead of the signal, it will not be necessary for the Signalman before lowering the signal, to wait until the man has returned to the train, but the Driver, when the signal is lowered, must proceed slowly to the box to enable the man to rejoin the train.

In the case of a rail motor or motor train, the Fireman must not allow the train to be moved until the Driver has rejoined it.

(*f*) Where appliances which require to be operated by Signalmen are provided to serve as a reminder that certain signals must not be lowered, the Signalman must make prompt use of such appliances, and the man who has gone to the signal box must return to the train after receiving an assurance that this has been done.

The appliance provided is a metal link or lever clip which must be placed over the lever of the signal protecting the train, and the Signalman must be careful not to remove the metal link or clip from the lever until the line affected is again clear.

> (NOTE.—**The placing of a metal link or clip on the lever working the signal at which a train is detained is not a protection for such train.**)

At some signal boxes special appliances are supplied to act as a reminder to the Signalman when the " Train out of section " or " Obstruction removed " signal must not be given for a train standing at the home signal, and the Driver, Fireman, Guard or Shunter, after being informed by the Signalman that the special appliance has been used, must return to the train.

(*g*) (i.) When a train has been brought to a stand owing to an automatic stop or semi-automatic stop signal being at Danger, the Driver must wait one minute or other prescribed period and except where special instructions are issued to the contrary communicate with the Signalman by telephone, inform him at which signal his train is detained and give description of his train. If it is necessary for the train to remain at the

D*

stop signal the Signalman must so advise the Driver and the Driver must communicate with the Signalman at intervals of not more than five minutes unless otherwise instructed.

If it is necessary owing to a failure of the signal or other emergency, for the train to pass at Danger an automatic stop signal, or a semi-automatic stop signal working automatically, authority will be given by the illumination of a " P " sign at the signal by the Signalman. Except as laid down in paragraph (ii.) of this clause and paragraph (i.) of clause (h) this indication will be the sole authority for the Driver to proceed.

If the signal at which the train is detained is a semi-automatic signal which is being controlled from a signal box or ground frame, the authority for the train to proceed past the signal at Danger will not be given by the illumination of the " P " sign, and Rules 37 (a) and 38 (a) and (b) will apply.

(ii.) If the Driver has been informed that the authority to pass the signal at Danger will be given by the illumination of the " P " sign, and after a further two minutes this sign is not illuminated, the Signalman must be so advised. If information is then received from the Signalman that he has operated the " P " sign switch, it must be assumed that the " P " sign has failed and the train may proceed in accordance with paragraph (iii.).

(iii.) In every case when a train proceeds past an automatic stop signal or semi-automatic stop signal working automatically, at Danger, in accordance with the preceding paragraph (i.) or (ii.) or clause (h) as the case may be, the Driver must give one long whistle and proceed cautiously as far as the line is clear towards the next stop signal in advance and at such a speed as to enable him to stop short of any obstruction.

The Driver must realise that the signal is possibly at Danger due to the presence of a train ahead, a broken or displaced rail, or an obstruction on the track, and he must therefore exercise the greatest caution.

In such cases if the next stop signal in advance, whether automatic or not, is not at Danger, the Driver must continue to proceed cautiously to the next stop signal beyond.

(iv.) When a train has been brought to a stand owing to an automatic or semi-automatic stop signal being at Danger and the Driver finds the " P " sign already illuminated, he must telephone to the Signalman and not accept the " P " sign as an authority to proceed until it has been extinguished and again illuminated.

(h) (i.) Should the telephone fail at an automatic stop signal at which a train is detained, the Fireman (or Guard, in the case of an electric train) must, unless special instructions to the contrary are in force, proceed to the nearest telephone in working order applicable to the line on which the train is standing, where he can communicate with the Signalman and act in accordance with clause (g), but if the Driver can see or ascertain that the line is clear to the next stop signal, he may proceed in accordance with paragraph (iii.) of clause (g) to such stop signal.

(ii.) Should the telephone fail at a semi-automatic stop signal at which a train is detained, the Fireman (or Guard, in the case of an electric train) must proceed to the signal box or ground frame and act in accordance with the instructions of the Signalman or person in charge, as the case may be. If, however, the signal box is closed or the ground frame is not in use, the Driver must act as shown in the preceding paragraph, after satisfying himself that any facing points or switch diamonds there may be between the signal at which his train is standing and the next stop signal are in the proper position for his train.

(*i*) **It will be the duty of the Driver, Fireman, Guard or Shunter, when he enters a signal box to remind the Signalman of the position of the train or vehicle in accordance with the instructions contained in clauses (*a*), (*b*) and (*c*) to insert in the train register book the time of his arrival with the remark " Rule 55," place his name against the entry, and to intimate clearly to the Signalman the title of the train he is protecting and on what line it is standing.**

(*j*) **Signalmen will be held responsible for seeing that the provisions of this Rule are carried out and for reporting any man failing to strictly observe it.**

(*k*) **The Provisions of Rule 55 do not apply as shown below :—**

> (i.) **On lines worked in accordance with the Regulations for Train Signalling by Permissive Block Telegraph (except where Firemen's call boxes are provided on such lines or in the case of passenger trains detained on goods lines or loops).**

(ii.) **On lines where station yard working is in operation (except where Firemen's call boxes are provided).**

(iii.) **On lines where "No Block or Bell" is in operation (except where Firemen's call boxes are provided).**

(iv.) **On dead-end lines at terminal stations or on dead-end bay lines at through stations.**

(v.) **On lines worked in accordance with the Regulations for Train Signalling by Telegraph Bells (except where Firemen's call boxes are provided or in the case of passenger trains detained on such lines).**

(vi.) **On goods loop lines entirely controlled by one signal box (except where Firemen's call boxes are provided on such lines, or in the case of passenger trains detained on such lines).**

(vii.) **In connection with trains not conveying passengers, or light engines, on goods lines worked in accordance with the Absolute Block Regulations, except where firemen's call boxes are provided. Should passenger trains be worked over such lines and be detained at signals, the rule must be carried out in all cases.**

55A. On lines used by passenger trains, when Trainmen have been advised by the Signalman that the block apparatus has failed and trains are being worked on the time interval system (i.e., there is no bell or speaking communication with the signal box ahead) track circuits or electrical depression bars provided at a home signal worked from the box ahead must not be relied upon by Trainmen to indicate the position of the train, and the following instructions must be carried out :—

(a) Should a train be brought to a stand owing to a home signal being at Danger, Rule 55, clause (a), must be immediately carried out unless appliances provided for Trainmen to communicate with the signal box can be made use of and an acknowledgment received.

(b) During fog or falling snow, should a train be detained owing to the outermost home signal being at Danger, the Guard must immediately apply the brake and go back not less than 100 yards in rear of his train and protect it by placing one detonator on the rail. After doing so he must at once rejoin his train. In the case of a light engine, the Fireman must carry out the duties of the Guard before complying with Rule 55, clause (a). In the case of a rail motor or motor train unaccompanied by a Guard or Shunter the train must first be similarly protected by the man whose duty it is to carry out Rule 55 as laid down in clause (c) of that Rule.

If a train is brought to a stand behind another train in the section, the rearmost train must be protected as previously described.

Drivers must not again start their trains after being brought to a stand, until sufficient time has been allowed for the man protecting the train to rejoin it.

(c) It will not be necessary for the Guard, Fireman or Shunter, as the case may be, to protect his train as prescribed in clause (b) in the following circumstances :—

  (i.) If a Handsignalman is on duty and the Trainman concerned is satisfied that he is protecting the train.

  (ii.) On single lines being worked by Electric Token, or Staff and Ticket, or Pilotman, provided the Driver is in possession of the electric token or staff or the Pilotman accompanies the train.

  (iii.) When the traffic of a double line is being worked over a single line of rails and the Pilotman accompanies the train.

(d) To enable the provisions of clauses (a) and (b) to be carried out, the Signalman must in addition to advising the Trainmen of the block failure also inform them that there is no communication with the signal box ahead.

1. V2 Class 2-6-2 No. 60810 at Woodford, 17 July 1964, beneath the sheer legs used for lifting. 'SC' on the smoke box door indicates 'self-cleaning', thus avoiding the ash having to be shovelled out. As some lines had received overhead electrification by this date, two white notices above the buffer beam warn of this danger. (Revd Alan Newman)

2. Shed scene at Bath, Green Park, 15 August 1949: Class 4F 0-6-0 No. 44523 left and Class 7F 2-8-0 right. Notice the overhead gantry for carrying ashes and the dilapidated state of the timber-built shed. (Author)

3. Ashes being raked from BR Standard Class 9F 2-10-0 No. 92214 at Bath Green Park around 1960. The coaling stage is on the right. (Dr T. R. N. Edwards)

4. Class 8F 2-8-0 No. 48336, a Willesden engine, below the ash plant at Bristol, Barrow Road, 30 June 1965. Inverted ash wagons are on the right. Beyond the ash plant is the coaling tower. (Revd Alan Newman)

5. BR Standard Class 5MT No. 73021 stands beneath Barrow Road ash plant, 9 June 1964, with a BR Standard Class 9F 2-10-0 No. 95152 to the right. The yard is still lit by gas lamps. (Revd Alan Newman)

6. Inspecting the smoke box of Class 5 4-6-0 No. 45065 at Nuneaton, 13 September 1965. Notice the hoods to carry smoke up through the roof. (Revd Alan Newman)

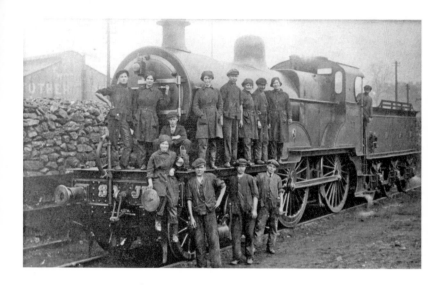

Left: 7. Oiling Battle of Britain Class 4-6-2 No. 34057 *Biggin Hill* at Bath Green Park, 5 March 1966. The long spout avoids the driver bending and also gives better access to parts not easily reached. (John Stamp)

Above: 8. Male and female cleaners on Somerset & Dorset Joint Railway 4-4-0 No. 71 at Bath during the First World War. The Whitaker tablet apparatus can be seen fixed to the tender. (Author's collection)

Above: 9. Passed fireman W. F. Grainger pretending to oil the big end. He is by the reversing rod of a Class 4F 0-6-0. On the splasher can be seen the plate 'LMS built 1928 Crewe'. (W. F. Grainger)

Right: 10. The crew working the GWR's Flying Dutchman broad gauge express around 1890. The driver has his hand on the regulator; on the tender behind him is the tool box. The GWR favoured right-hand drive, but some other companies preferred the left. (Author's collection)

11. View of a GWR cab: the combined (steam and vacuum) brake handle, upper left; regulator, lower left; screw reverser in mid-gear, lower right, and the Automatic Train Control and bell, right. Below is a small vacuum reservoir. A three-sight lubricator is to the left of the top of the reverser. (M. J. Tozer)

12. Lancashire & Yorkshire Railway 0-6-0 No. 1300 on the Avon Valley Railway at Bitton, 1 July 1999. The regulator handle shows in front of the spectacle glass; the injector valves can be seen and two water gauges. Notice how airy the cab is – very pleasant on a hot day, but not so good in the winter. The combined number plate and builder's plate reads, 'L&Y Ry. Co. Makers Horwich. 1896.' (Author)

13. A boilersmith enters, or leaves, the firebox of an LMS 4-6-0 in 1936. Notice the ventilator in the cab roof; the regulator, centre, with the handle going left, as it is a left-hand drive engine. The blower handle is directly below the regulator and handy for use by either driver or fireman. The steam manifold allows just one hole in the boiler to feed the injectors, carriage heating, whistles and boiler pressure gauge. The screw reverser is on the left. A plate shields the driver's legs from the heat emitted from the firebox. A handle opens the firebox doors. (Author's collection)

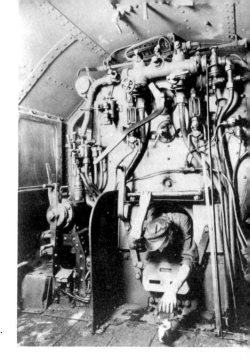

14. The cab of a London & North Western Railway Webb compound locomotive: the fire hole, centre, with the regulator above and the reverser wheel on the left. The two small wheels operate the injectors. There is but one water gauge. Notice there is not much room to swing a shovel. The coupling bar for the tender is supplemented by two rings. Below are pipes from the tender to feed each injector. (Author's collection)

15. E1 Class 0-6-0T No. 4 *Wroxall* at Newport, Isle of Wight. Notice the sheeting on the bunker to enlarge the coal capacity; the Westinghouse air brake pump on the cab side and the air reservoir below the bunker. Behind the bunker is the tool box. The whistle is on the roof. (Author's collection)

16. Facilities were sometimes more primitive on industrial lines: the driver has to climb a ladder to control the water supply, while the fireman holds the hose. *Major* is an Andrew Barclay 0-4-0ST at Irchester Ironstone Quarries, 20 March 1964. (Revd Alan Newman)

17. LNWR 0-6-0 No. 1351 has come to grief, but enables us to see the water pick-up apparatus on the underside of the tender. (Author's collection)

18. 4-6-0 No. 7813 *Freshford Manor* near the coal stage, Bath Green Park, 13 May 1961. Notice the neat way the front coupling has been hooked. The ATC (automatic train control) equipment can be seen below the front axle. (Revd Alan Newman)

19. Class 7F 0-8-0 No. 49406 beneath the coaling plant, Birkenhead, 17 August 1960. No. 49406 is fitted with a tender cab to make conditions rather more pleasant when driving in reverse. (Revd Alan Newman)

20. Ivatt Class 2MT No. 41291, partly on the turntable at Templecombe, being coaled by hand crane, 6 December 1965, while the driver is oiling its motion. (Revd Alan Newman)

Right: 21. Two guards at Bath: Frank Staddon, left; holding a shunter's pole, and Jack Lake, right. (R. J. Coles)
Below: 22. BR Standard Class 4MT 2-6-0 No. 76015 on the turntable at Bath Green Park, 25 May 1957. The crew is turning a handle. (Revd Alan Newman)

23. Ex-Somerset & Dorset Class 4 0-6-0 No. 44558 being turned at Bath Green Park, 7 June 1964. Two water tanks are beyond BR Standard Class 9F 2-10-0 No. 92214. (Author)

24. Bristol Barrow Road, 12 March 1965, when it was also shared by ex-GWR locomotives. Left to right: 8750 Class 0-6-0PT No. 3696 fitted with a snow plough; No. 9623 and No. 9680. Lighting is by gas. (Revd Alan Newman)

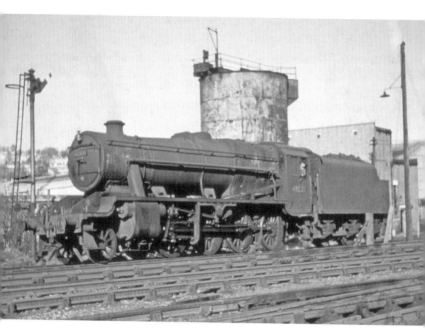

25. LMS Class 8F 2-8-0 No. 48525 built by the LNER at Doncaster, seen here beside the water softener, Bath Green Park. (R. J. Cannon)

26. Class 7F 2-8-0 No. 53807 being coaled at Bath Green Park, 7 June 1964. An ash wagon stands on the right. (Author)

Above: 27. BR Standard Class 4MT 2-6-0 No. 76026 working the 1.10 p.m. Bournemouth West to Bristol Temple Meads, 1 June 1963, takes on water at Blandford Forum. (Author)

Left: 28. West Country Class Pacific No. 34006 *Bude* being wound round on the turntable at Bath Green Park shed, 5 March 1966. (Author)

Above: 29. Longmoor Military Railway ex-War Department 2-10-0 No. 600 *Gordon* at the open day on 28 September 1968. It is in a superb condition. To help ease it round tight curves, the centre driving wheel is flangeless. (Revd Alan Newman)

Right: 30. A re-railing demonstration of ex-WD 2-10-0 No. 601 during the Longmoor open day on 3 June 1967. No. 601 was lifted vertically and then pushed horizontally by hydraulic power supplied by a portable generator. The disc pony truck wheel was a feature of the austerity design. (Author)

31. The smoke box and cylinder of Class 8F 2-8-0 No. 48309 at Bath Green Park locomotive depot on 4 April 1965. The van in the background lettered 'MP Bath' belongs to the breakdown train. (Author)

32. The ex-Huntley & Palmer's fireless locomotive No. 1. Periodically it was supplied with steam from a stationary boiler. It is seen here on 6 July 1974 at the one-time Somerset & Dorset Railway Trust's Museum at Radstock. (Author)

DETENTION OF TRAINS ON RUNNING LINES.
Rule 55.

(a) When a train has been brought to a stand owing to a stop signal being at Danger, the Driver must sound the engine whistle, and, if still detained, the Guard, Shunter or Fireman must (except as shewn in the following paragraph, or where printed instructions are given to the contrary) go to the signal box and remind the Signalman of the position of the train, and, except as provided in clause (f), remain in the box until permission is obtained for the train to proceed. In clear weather a train must not stand more than three minutes at a stop signal before the man goes to the signal box, During fog or falling snow, unless the stop signal is lowered immediately after the engine whistle has been sounded, the man must **at once proceed** to the signal box.

In the case of single lines, if the Driver is in possession of the train staff or electrc token, it will not be necessary for the man to go to the signal box to remind the Signalman of the position of the train in connection with trains detained at home signals.

Track circuits.

Where track circuits or electrical depression bars are provided, as indicated on or near the signal posts, or in respect to which printed instructions are issued, and the train is standing on such track circuits or bars, it will not be necessary for the Guard, Shunter or Fireman to go to the signal box to remind the signalman of the position of the train, but on lines used by passenger trains when the trainmen have been advised that the block apparatus has failed and that trains are being worked on the time interval system, these track circuits and electrical depression bars provided at a home signal worked by the box ahead, must not be relied upon by trainmen to indicate the position of the train, and should a train be brought to a stand at a home signal Rule 55 clause (a) must immediately be carried out unless appliances provided for trainmen to communicate with the signal box can be made use of and an acknowledgment received. Where other appliances are provided for the purpose of communicating with the Signalman, the Guard, Shunter or Fireman must immediately make use of such appliances, but if an acknowledgement is not received the provisions of the preceding paragraph must be carried out (See L.M.S. and Southern Amendments at the end of this Rule).

Shunting movements.

(b) When a train or vehicle has passed a stop signal for the purpose of being crossed to another line, or to be let into a siding, or has been shunted onto the opposite running line, or placed on either a main or branch line at a junction, or when a train or vehicle has been shunted from a siding onto a running line for the purpose of being crossed to another line, the Guard, Shunter or Fireman must (except where printed instructions are given to the contrary), when the train or vehicle comes to a stand, and is detained, **proceed immediately** to the signal box and remind the Signalman of the position of the train or vehicle, and, except as provided in clause (f), remain in the box until the Signalman can give permission for it to proceed or to be shunted clear of the running lines.

(c) The duty of going to the signal box must (except in the case of rail motors, motor trains and electric trains) be performed by the Guard, Shunter or Fireman who is nearest to the signal box.

Shunting from one line to another.

(d) When a train or vehicle has been shunted from one running line to another, the Guard, Shunter or Fireman, as the case may be, must, before going to the signal box, satisfy himself that the line from which the train or vehicle has been shunted is clear.

Trainmen joining train.

Sufficient time must be allowed for the Guard, Shunter or Fireman to rejoin the train before the signal is lowered, and the Driver must not, when the signal is lowered, go forward until he has received a hand signal from the Guard or Shunter to intimate that he has rejoined the train. By day the hand signal must be given by holding one arm above the head or the waving of a green flag above the head, and by night a green light held steadily above the head.

If the signal box is ahead of the signal, it will not be necessary for the Signalman, before lowering the signal, to wait until the man has returned to the train, but the Driver, when the signal is lowered, must proceed slowly to the box to enable the man to rejoin the train (See L.M.S. Amendment at end of this Rule).

Appliances in signal boxes.

(f) Where appliances which require to be operated by Signalmen are provided to serve as a reminder that certain signals must not be lowered, the man who has gone to the signal box must return to the train after receiving an assurance that this has been done.

Automatic stop signals.

When a Driver finds an automatic stop signal at Danger, he must bring his train **to a stand,** and if a telephone is provided at the signal communicate at once with the Signalman and act in accordance with his instructions. Should he receive instructions to pass the signal at **Danger** he must give **one long whistle and proceed cautiously** as far as the line is clear or to the next stop signal in advance at such a speed as to enable him to stop short of any obstruction there may be. If the telephone is out of order, or a telephone is not provided at the signal, and the Danger indication is not changed, the Driver must **wait one minute** or other prescribed period, give **one long whistle,** and then proceed **cautiously** as above directed. (This is the well-known "Stop and Proceed" Rule.)

In such circumstances, if the next stop signal in advance, whether automatic or not, is in the Caution or Clear position, the Driver must continue to proceed cautiously to the next stop signal beyond.

Whenever a Driver has passed an **automatic stop signal at Danger** under the circumstances mentioned above he must so **inform the Signalman at the next box in advance,** unless he has been previously instructed by the Signalman to pass the signal at Danger.

Semi-automatic signals.

Stop signals designated "semi-automatic" must **not be passed at Danger,** except in accordance with Rules 37 (a) and 38 (a) and (b), or where specially authorised.

When a train has been brought to a stand owing to a stop signal being at Danger and the signal bears a sign as shewn in diagram No. 1 it will not be necessary for the Guard, Shunter or Fireman to go to the signal box to remind the Signalman of the position of the train.

G.W.R. Addition to this rule.—

At a number of signals either track circuiting, fouling bars, or reply push bells have been provided to remind Signalmen of the presence of trains or engines, and it is consequently unnecessary at these places for Trainmen to go to the signal box to carry out the provisions of Rule 55.

White enamelled notice plates, diamond shaped, or "Bell to Box" indicators (see page 60 for illustrations) have been provided at or near these signals as a reminder to Trainmen that they need not go to the signal box to inform the Signalman of the position of the train or engine except that the engine whistle must be sounded in accordance with the Rule.

If a train is detained at a signal in connection with which a reply push bell is fixed, it will be necessary for the Fireman to alight and press the bell push and obtain an answering ring from the Signalman as an acknowledgement. If the answering ring is not, however, forthcoming, the Fireman must proceed to the signal box to carry out the provisions of Rule 55.

L.M.S Company's amendment to clause (a).—

Signalman to be reminded.

(a) (i.) When a train has been brought to a stand owing to a stop signal being at Danger, the Driver must sound the engine whistle, and, if the signal is not immediately lowered, the Guard, Shunter or Fireman must (except as shewn in paragraphs (ii.) and (iii.) of this clause), at once go to the signal box and remind the Signalman of the position of the train, and, except as provided in clause (f), remain in the box until permission is obtained for the train to proceed.

Track circuits or other appliances.

(ii.) If the signal bears a sign as shewn in diagram No. 2, the Fireman, or, in cases where vehicles are in front of the engine, the Guard or Shunter, must at once press the plunger fixed on the signal post or on a pillar near by. (Page 60).

When the stop signal bears a sign as shewn in diagram No. 1, Trainmen need not go to the signal box to carry out Rule 55. (Page 60).

Except where the indication "RULE 55 EXEMPT —PRESS KEY" is given, the sounding of the bell at the signal post or pillar in response to the plunger being pressed is an indication that the signal so given has been effective and it will not be necessary for the Fireman, Guard or Shunter to go to the signalbox to remind the Signalman of the position of the train, but, if the bell does not sound, the instructions respecting the Fireman, Guard or Shunter going to the signal box to remind the

Signalman of the position of the train must be carried out. Where the indication "RULE 55 EXEMPT — PRESS KEY" is given at the signal post or pillar, the plunger must be operated at once and this will indicate in the signal box the position of the train without a bell sounding at the signal post or pillar. In such cases it will not be necessary for the Fireman, Guard or Shunter to go to the signal box to remind the Signalman of the position of the train after the plunger has been pressed.

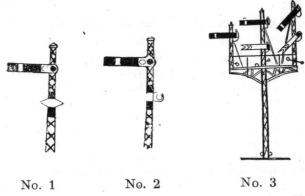

No. 1   No. 2   No. 3

In some cases the signs shewn in diagrams No. 1 and No. 2 are illuminated or the actual position of the Fireman's call box is indicated by a lamp which is illuminated during darkness.

The signals on No. 3 Gantry are NOT EXEMPT from the provisions of Rule 55.

In cases where a train has been brought to a stand at a stop signal and the man responsible for carrying out this Rule has operated the plunger of the instrument provided, and the Signalman then lowers the signal for the engine, or engine and part of the train to draw forward for shunting operations or any other cause leaving part of the train on the running line, the plunger must again be operated by the person responsible for the rear part of the train when the engine or engine and part of the train has passed the stop signal and it has been placed to Danger.

The appliances and indicators referred to in this paragraph (ii.) must not be taken as applying to a train or vehicle which has been shunted onto the opposite running line, or has come to a stand after making any movement other than proceeding along the right running line in its ordinary course; in such circumstances, the man responsible for carrying out this Rule must in all cases proceed immediately to the signal box as laid down in clause (b).

L.M.S. Company's amendment to second paragraph of clause (e).—

Except as shewn below, if the signal box is ahead of the signal, it will not be necessary for the Signalman, before lowering the signal, to wait until the man has returned to the train, but the Driver, when the signal is lowered, must proceed slowly to the box to enable the man to rejoin the train.

In the case of a rail motor or motor train, the Fireman must not allow the train to be moved until the Driver has rejoined it.

L.M.S. Company's additions to Rule.—

It will be the duty of the Driver, Fireman, Guard or Shunter, when he enters a signal box to remind the Signalman of the position of the train or vehicle in accordance with the instructions contained in clauses (a), (b) and (c), to insert in the train register or other book provided the time of his arrival with the remark "Rule 55," place his name against the entry, and to intimate clearly to the Signalman the title of the train he is protecting and on what line it is standing.

The provisions of Rule 55 must be carried out on lines worked on the Absolute Block Telegraph System or on lines worked in accordance with the General Regulations for Train Signalling by Telegraph Bells, but do not apply as shewn below:—

(i) (Except where Firemen's call boxes are provided on such lines or in the case of passenger trains detained on goods lines or loops, or such lines); On lines worked in accordance with the Regulations for Train Signalling by Permissive Block Telegraph, or the General Regulations for Train Signalling by Telegraph Bells, also on goods Loop Lines entirely controlled by one signal box.

(ii.) On lines where station yard working is in operation (except where Firemen's call boxes are provided).

(iii.) On lines where "No Block or Bell" is in operation (except where Firemen's call boxes are provided).

(iv.) On dead-end lines at terminal stations or on dead-end bay lines at through stations.

(v.) In connection with trains not conveying passengers, or light engines, on goods lines worked in accordance with the Absolute Block Regulations, except where Firemen's boxes are provided. The Rule must be applied when passenger trains working over such lines are detained at signals.

Southern Company's addition to Rule.—

Rule 55 will not apply on dead-end lines at terminal stations or on dead-end bay lines at through stations.

The sign indicating exemption from the provisions of Rule 55 on lines other than those mentioned above and in the third paragraph of clause (a) of this Rule, consists of a white enamelled plate, shaped thus:— ⟨⟩ fixed on the signal post, and in the case of trains detained at signals equipped with these signs the Guard or Fireman need not go to the signal box to remind the Signalman of the position of the train, except as provided in Rule 55a. The engine whistle must, however, be sounded in accordance with the first paragraph of Rule 55 unless printed instructions are given to the contrary.

The sign described above, when fixed on the post of a running signal, applies to through movements only and in the event of a shunting movement being detained thereat, the provisions of clauses (a) to (f) inclusive of Rule 55 must be observed.

The provisions of clauses (a) to (f) inclusive of Rule 55 must also be observed in connection with all other shunting movements, except where the movement is controlled by a ground signal equipped with a similar sign to that indicated above, in which case it will only be necessary for the Driver to sound the engine whistle when detained thereat.

5

DETONATORS

Detonators are valuable devices for attracting the attention of trainmen. Devised by E. A. Cooper in 1841, they consist of a flat, disc-shaped metal box containing a small explosive charge. They may be fixed to a rail surface by soft metal straps. A wheel passing over a detonator causes an explosion.

In the event of an accident or breakdown, a guard will walk back and lay detonators to protect his train, while if the other road has been fouled, the fireman will walk forward to lay detonators to protect the front of his train. In fog or falling snow, when semaphore signals cannot be seen, a fogman lays detonators and exhibits a coloured lamp to indicate the position of a distant signal.

56. Detonators are used for the purpose of attracting the attention of Trainmen. They must be placed as nearly as possible in the centre of the rail, and when fixed by hand they must be securely fastened by bending the clips round the upper flanges of the rail.

57. (a) Drivers, Guards, Signalmen, Crossing Keepers, Gangers and Fogsignalmen must be provided

with detonators, which they must always have ready for use when on duty, and they will be held responsible for keeping a proper supply.

(*b*) Station Masters must maintain a sufficient stock of detonators and keep a supply in a suitable place easy of access and known to all persons connected with the station.

58. (*a*) Detonators must be carefully handled as they are liable to explode if roughly treated.

(*b*) They must be kept in dry places and not left in contact with brick walls, damp wood, chloride of lime or other disinfectant, nor exposed to the action of steam or other vapour.

(*c*) The month and year of manufacture is shown on the label outside each packet and is stamped on each detonator. Detonators must be issued in the order of the dates stamped on them ; those of the oldest date being always used first.

(*d*) The stock (including loose detonators and those supplied to Drivers, Guards, Signalmen, Crossing Keepers, Gangers and Fogsignalmen, also any kept in Guards' brake vans) must be examined during the first week in March and the first week in September. Detonators must be returned to the Stores Department at once if bearing any signs of rust on the outside of the case, or appearing unsatisfactory in any way. Except where instructions are issued to the contrary they must be returned to the Stores Department at the expiration of three years from the date stamped upon them. At places where authority is given to use detonators up to five years old, they must be returned to the Stores Department at the expiration of that period. Detonators must not under any circumstances be used after they are five years old.

When a packet of detonators is opened, the whole of them must be examined, and should any show signs of rust none of them must be used, but the whole packet must be sent to the Stores Department.

(e) Should any detonator fail to explode the circumstance must be promptly reported to the **Chief Operating Manager, or in the case of the Northern Division, the Chief Officer for Scotland,** and the defective detonator forwarded to him for examination.

59. (a) When one or more detonators are exploded by a train at stop signals or signal boxes, the Driver must immediately bring his train to a stand, whether a hand signal is exhibited or not, unless he receives a green hand signal waved slowly from side to side in which case he must reduce speed as laid down in the second paragraph of Rule 60, or he receives a yellow hand signal at a three-aspect signal when he must reduce speed and be prepared to find the next stop signal at Danger.

(b) When a detonator is exploded at a distant signal and a yellow hand signal is exhibited, the Driver must be prepared to stop at the home signal. Should, however, he receive a hand Danger signal in addition to the explosion of the detonator, he must, unless he is satisfied the hand signal is given for the purpose of repeating a distant signal at Caution, in clear weather bring his train under such complete control as to enable him to stop at once if required, and then proceed cautiously to the place of obstruction or until he receives a further signal for his guidance ; during fog or falling snow he must bring his train to a stand and then proceed cautiously to the place of obstruction, or until he receives a further signal for his guidance.

When a detonator is exploded at a distant signal but a green hand signal held steadily is exhibited or in the absence of any hand signal, the Driver must be entirely guided by the detonator, and act in the same way as if a Caution hand signal had been exhibited.

60. When one or more detonators are exploded by a train other than at a fixed signal or at a signal box whether accompanied by a hand Danger signal or not the Driver must, in clear weather, bring his train under such complete control as to enable him to stop at once if required and then proceed cautiously to the place of obstruction or until he receives a further signal for his guidance ; during fog or falling snow he must bring his train to a stand and then proceed cautiously to the place of obstruction or until he receives a further signal for his guidance.

If after the explosion of a detonator, the Driver receives a green hand signal waved slowly from side to side he must reduce the speed of his train to 15 miles per hour, or such other reduced speed as may be prescribed, over the portion of the line to which such green hand signal applies.

6

SIGNALLING DURING PERIODS OF POOR VISIBILITY

As we have seen in the case of the Abbots Ripton accident, safe railway working depends on signals being observed and obeyed. In order to minimise problems caused by fog and falling snow, rules were devised. Before the passing of the Clean Air Act of 1956, brought in as a result of the Great Smog of 1952, sometimes fog could be so thick that even when a train was standing at the foot of a signal the arm could not be seen and the fireman had to climb the ladder to ascertain its position.

When fog obscured a certain mark from a signal box, known as a 'fogging point', the signalman called out fogmen to go to his distant signals and fix a detonator on the rail if it showed 'Danger' and remove it when it displayed 'Clear'. This detonator was placed in advance of the signal to alert the driver and give him a chance to observe both it and also any hand signal displayed by the fogman. A small hut and brazier was usually provided for the fogman and if there were multiple tracks, in order to avoid the danger of a fogman crossing lines in poor visibility, by using a lever placed in his hut, he could place a detonator. Fogmen were usually platelayers.

If no fogman was available, a signalman could not accept a train until both his section and the one ahead were clear – in other words, there was a double block between trains.

Particularly in busy commuter areas, special fog timetables came into operation, some freight trains being cancelled and the number of passenger trains reduced. The rules regarding train working in fog were so successful that no accident in the twentieth century could be attributed to fog in a mechanical signalled area.

SIGNALLING DURING FOG OR FALLING SNOW.

84. The Station Master must arrange beforehand with the Permanent-way Inspector the allocation of the Permanent-way men who are to act as Fog-signalmen at the various posts. If there are insufficient Permanent-way men for the purpose the Station Master must report accordingly to his superior officer.

A regular Fogsignalman, and where necessary a relief Fogsignalman, must be appointed for every fogging post and a list of the names and addresses of these men showing the post to which each man is assigned must be exhibited in a conspicuous position in the Station Master's office and signal box.

The Ganger or other person referred to in Rule 221 must not be assigned a fixed post, but must be left free to examine the line in accordance with that Rule.

He may, however, when no other competent man is available, be employed to call Fogsignalmen, to visit them at their posts, and distribute detonators as required.

85. A sufficient supply of detonators, hand lamps, and flags for the use of the Fogsignalmen must be kept at stations and signal boxes in connection with which the men are employed.

86. During fog or falling snow the Station Master must satisfy himself that the Fogsignalmen have proceeded to the posts where their services are required.

87. (a) When a fog or snowstorm occurs during the normal working hours of the men appointed to act as Fogsignalmen they must at once report to the Signalman and take his instructions. The Signalman must advise the Station Master if any Fogsignalman fails to report for duty.

When it is necessary to employ Fogsignalmen outside their normal working hours the Station Master or Signalman must, unless the men have been previously notified, arrange to have them called and sent to their respective posts, but any Fogsignalman who becomes aware that his services are required must report for duty without waiting to be called.

(b) If a Fogsignalman, proceeding to the signal box to report for duty, has to pass the signal to which he is appointed, he must, if that signal is at Danger, or Caution in the case of a distant signal, place one detonator on the rail of the line to which the signal applies and then proceed to the signal box, getting back to his post as promptly as possible. He must keep a few detonators in his possession for the purpose of this Rule.

(c) When a Fogsignalman has to pass a signal box on his way to take up duty at a signal worked from another box, he must inform the Signalman that he is going to commence fogsignalling at such signal, and the Signalman so informed must advise the Signalman at the box from which the signal is worked that the Fogsignalman has gone to his post, and at what time. It will not then be necessary for the Fogsignalman to proceed to the box from which the signal is worked. In such cases the Fogsignalman's equipment must be kept at the box at which he reports.

(d) When the fog has cleared sufficiently, or the snowstorm has ceased, the Fogsignalman must place one detonator on the rail of the line to which the signal applies, and then go to the nearest signal box and ascertain whether his services are still required. If the signal for which he is fogsignalling is worked from another box the Signalman must obtain this information from the Signalman at that box.

NOTE.—*On the Great Western Railway 2 detonators, 10 yards apart, are used to carry out Rules* 87, 90, 91 *and* 92, *except* :—

(i.) *Where automatic train control is in operation* (1 *detonator*).
(ii.) *Where a Fogsignalman is employed in connection with a stop signal* (3 *detonators*, 6 *feet apart*).

88.   Persons responsible for the provision of relief

Fogsignalmen must arrange for these men to be called as required.

89. Signalmen must enter in the train register book the time each Fogsignalman commences and leaves duty.

90. Before proceeding to his post each Fogsignal-man must be supplied with 36 detonators, or more if necessary, a hand signal lamp, trimmed and lighted, and a red, a yellow (where necessary), and a green flag.

If the stock of detonators first supplied is likely to become soon exhausted, the Fogsignalman must obtain a further supply from the nearest station or signal box. Should the Fogsignalman have to leave his post for this purpose, he must leave one detonator on the rail.

NOTE.—*On the Great Western Railway 2 detonators, 10 yards apart, are used to carry out Rules 87, 90, 91 and 92, except* :—

(i.) *Where automatic train control is in operation (1 detonator).*
(ii.) *Where a Fogsignalman is employed in connection with a stop signal (3 detonators, 6 feet apart).*

91. (*a*) A Fogsignalman employed at a distant signal must place himself outside the signal, and in such a position as will enable him to keep the signal, or its repeater, well in sight.

Immediately after the passing of a train the Fog-signalman must place one detonator on the rail of the line to which the signal applies, and keep it there so long as the signal is at Caution and exhibit a hand Caution signal, held steadily, to the Driver and

Guard of an approaching train. When the signal is lowered he must remove the detonator from the rail and exhibit to the Driver and Guard a green hand signal, held steadily. On single lines the detonator must be removed from the rail when the Fogsignalman is satisfied that a train is approaching from the opposite direction ; in such case, a hand signal must not be given and the detonator must be replaced immediately after the passage of the train.

(b) The Fogsignalman must see that the distant signal which has been lowered for a train to pass is replaced at Caution after the passing of the train. If, after a reasonable time has elapsed, the signal is not replaced at Caution, the Fogsignalman must leave the detonator on the rail, and if employed at a signal near to a signal box advise the Signalman of the occurrence. If he is not able to communicate with the Signalman he must go back along the line affected showing a red hand signal and place on the rail 3 detonators, 10 yards apart, as far as is necessary to ensure the next train being brought to a stand at the distant signal ; after placing the detonators on the rail the Fogsignalman must immediately return to his post continuing to exhibit the red hand signal. When the train has stopped, the Driver must be instructed to proceed cautiously and inform the Signalman at the box in advance of the circumstances. Subsequent trains must be similarly dealt with until the signal has been replaced at Caution, or the Fogsignalman is satisfied that Drivers are being advised by the Signalman at the box in rear that the distant signal is not working properly. When the Fogsignalman is so satisfied he must keep a detonator on the rail and exhibit a hand Caution signal until the distant signal is again in working order. In the case of single lines, should a train travelling in the opposite direction explode the 3 detonators referred to above the Fogsignalman must replace them.

The same steps must be taken in the event of a distant signal light going out, and the Fogsignalman not being able to relight the lamp.

A Fogsignalman finding the distant signal in the Clear position upon arrival at his post must satisfy himself that the signal is working properly.

(c) When the distant signal is on the same post as a stop signal and the stop signal is at Danger a red hand signal must be exhibited by the Fogsignalman and he must not take up the detonator unless both signals are lowered. Should the stop signal be lowered and the distant signal remain at Caution, the Fogsignalman must exhibit a hand Caution signal, and if the fog is so dense that the Driver cannot see the distant signal the Fogsignalman must verbally caution him by using the words " Home signal off—distant on," or " Starting (or advanced starting) signal off—distant on," as the case may be.

Where a Fogsignalman is provided at the stop signals at a Junction or other diverging point where a distant signal or signals are provided under such stop signals for one or more routes, but not for all routes, the Fogsignalman must, if such distant signal or signals are not applicable to the route for which a stop signal has been lowered,

take up the detonator as soon as the stop signal for such diverging route is lowered. The Fog-signalman must, if practicable, verbally advise the Driver for which route the stop signal is " off " but, in such circumstances, no hand signal should be given.

(d) If the Fogsignalman becomes aware of any obstruction on the line or lines in the immediate neighbourhood of the signal for which he is signalling other than from a train not having gone forward, he must leave the detonator on the rail and at once take the necessary steps to protect such obstruction in accordance with Rules 179, clause (a), and 181, after which he must return to his post at the distant signal. If the Fogsignalman is employed at a signal near to a signal box, he must also take steps to advise the Signalman of the occurrence.

(e) When a Fogsignalman is employed in connection with a stop signal he must, when the signal is at Danger, place one detonator on the rail of the line affected, exhibit a red hand signal to the Driver of an approaching train, and carry out any instructions he may receive from the Signalman. When the signal is lowered to the Clear position the Fogsignalman must remove the detonator from the rail and exhibit a green hand signal to the Driver and Guard.

In the case of a three-position semaphore signal in the Caution position or a multiple-aspect signal exhibiting the aspect one yellow or two yellows, he must keep the detonator on the rail and exhibit a yellow hand signal to the Driver and Guard.

Fogsignalmen are not employed in multiple-aspect signal areas unless otherwise specially advised.

(*f*) Where a calling-on signal or shunt-ahead signal is provided, the Fogsignalman, when employed at such signal, must exhibit a hand Danger signal and maintain the detonator on the rail whilst the signals are at Danger. When the calling-on or shunt-ahead signal is lowered, he must, whether there be a distant signal, or not, fixed under the stop signal, maintain the detonator on the rail and verbally caution the Driver by using the words " Calling-on signal off," or " Shunt-ahead signal off," as the case may be, and after obtaining the Driver's acknowledgment withdraw the hand Danger signal.

Where a warning signal is provided, whether there is a distant signal or not on the same post, the Fogsignalman must, when employed at such signal, exhibit a hand Danger signal and maintain a detonator on the rail whilst the signals are at Danger. When the warning signal is lowered he must exhibit a hand Caution signal, maintain the detonator on the rail, and verbally caution the Driver, using the words " Warning signal off."

(*g*) The Fogsignalman must see that the stop, calling-on, shunt-ahead or warning signal, as the case may be, is replaced at Danger after the passing of each train ; if, however, the signal is not replaced at Danger, the Fogsignalman must put down one detonator, and at once communicate with the Signalman.

Note.—*On the Great Western Railway 2 detonators, 10 yards apart, are used to carry out Rules 87, 90, 91 and 92, except :—*

(i.) *Where automatic train control is in operation (1 detonator).*

(ii.) *Where a Fogsignalman is employed in connection with a stop signal (3 detonators, 6 feet apart).*

92. (*a*) After having fixed the detonator on the rail, the Fogsignalman must stand in the best position, having regard to his own safety, for effectively giving the hand signals to the Driver and Guard.

(*b*) When one man is fogsignalling for two or more lines it will not always be practicable for the Fogsignalman to exhibit the prescribed hand signals, in which case the provisions of Rule 59 must be observed.

(*c*) When the fixed signal for which he is fogsignalling cannot be seen by the Fogsignalman, he must, unless he can satisfy himself to the contrary, assume that it is at Danger, or Caution in the case of a distant signal.

(*d*) In cases of accident, failure, or obstruction, Guards and Drivers must act strictly in accordance with the prescribed Rules, and must not depend upon Fogsignalmen for the protection of their trains.

NOTE.—*On the Great Western Railway 2 detonators, 10 yards apart, are used to carry out Rules 87, 90, 91 and 92, except* :—

(i.) *Where automatic train control is in operation (1 detonator).*

(ii.) *Where a Fogsignalman is employed in connection with a stop signal (3 detonators, 6 feet apart).*

93. Where the Fogsignalmen are numerous, a competent man must be appointed to visit them at their posts, to see that they are properly performing their duties, and are supplied with the necessary equipment and to furnish them with a further supply of detonators if required.

94. When the Signalman requires to stop an approaching train during fog or falling snow and a Fogsignalman is not on duty, he must keep his signals at Danger, and, when practicable, place one detonator on the rail of the line to which the signals apply.

At signal boxes where emergency detonator placers are provided, the provisions of this Rule must always be carried out during fog or falling snow whether a Fogsignalman is on duty or not.

NOTE.—*On the Great Western Railway two detonators, 10 yards apart, are used to carry out this Rule.*

95. (a) During severe frost or falling snow, signals, points, locks and bars, must be frequently worked by the Signalman when the section is clear and no train has been signalled, in order to prevent frost or snow impeding the working of such apparatus.

(b) Fogsignalmen must see that nothing interferes with the true working of the arms and lights of the signals for which they are fogsignalling ; that the signal arms, lamp glasses and spectacles are kept clear from snow ; and, as far as practicable, that the wires work freely over the pulleys. The Fogsignalmen must at once report to the Signalman any defect in the signals or impediment to their proper working.

7

WORKING IN STATION YARDS

Although generally only one train is allowed in a section at a time, there are exceptions, one being when vehicles need to be shunted to the rear of a train, or when a very long platform is used for coping with two trains. This is called 'permissive working'.

STATION YARD WORKING.

96. At a terminal station, dead end bay, or where specially authorised at a through station where the entrance to and exit from a platform line is controlled by one signal box, a train may be allowed to enter such platform line when it is already occupied by another train or vehicles provided the line is clear to the point to which the train has to run, but in such circumstances, or if the Signalman is in doubt as to whether the line is clear, he must stop the train at the signal controlling the entrance to that line, and after lowering the signal exhibit a green hand signal held steadily. Where a subsidiary signal is provided this must be used instead of giving the green hand signal.

97. When a train is allowed to proceed towards the rear of another train which is moving forward, the Driver of the second train must follow cautiously and at such a distance as will enable him to avoid colliding with the first train in the event of it being stopped, and he must not pass a signal which has been lowered for the first train until it has been replaced to Danger and again lowered.

98. When a signal is lowered for a train to leave a station or siding to run towards a train ahead of such signal, the Driver must proceed at such a speed as will enable him to stop before reaching the train ahead.

8

LEVEL CROSSINGS

The Highways Act of 1839 required railway level crossings to have gates attended by 'good and proper persons'. Earlier Acts required gates to be kept closed across the road, but the Regulation of Railways Act of 1842 and the Railway Clauses Act of 1845 empowered the Board of Trade to authorise exceptions and eventually it became customary for gates to be normally kept closed across a railway.

There are three main types of level crossing: foot; accommodation or occupation; and public highway. Today, with diesel and electric trains running at higher speeds and less visible than steam trains, foot crossings are being eliminated by diversion of footpaths, or providing a bridge or underpass.

Accommodation or occupation crossings were provided when a railway severed property and such a crossing facilitated access. Under the 1845 Act gates at these crossings faced outwards and did not block the railway, responsibility for shutting them securely resting with the user. As with foot crossings, modern conditions have made such crossings more dangerous than in the past, especially as machinery can become grounded on a crossing which, although itself level, may have a steep slope to the side.

Busier public highway crossings often had a subsidiary wicket gate available to pedestrians after the road gates had been closed, then shortly before a train arrived, the signalman pulled a lever to lock them. These wicket gates were also used by cyclists pushing their machines and on at least one occasion, a cyclist used the front wheel to hold the gate open for a friend though the train was approaching; he ignored a warning call from the signalman to remove the wheel, the signalman pulled the locking lever and the gate closed, buckling the cycle's front wheel.

The gates of busy level crossings were operated from the signal box by turning a hand-wheel. In some locations the signalman had a job finding a gap in the traffic to operate the wheel. One such place was Radstock, south of Bath, particularly busy on summer Saturdays as, in pre-motorway days, the A367 was one of the main routes from the Midlands to the South West. The Somerset & Dorset Railway was also particularly busy on such days and if vehicles were not held up at the S&D level crossing, they were likely to be delayed by the parallel GWR level crossing a few yards away.

Occupation crossings were generally surfaced with timber sleepers, as were many road crossings, but some of the latter in towns were surfaced with stone setts.

LEVEL CROSSINGS.

99. Unless special authority be given to the contrary, the gates at level crossings must be kept closed across the roadway, except when required to be opened to allow the line to be crossed.

100. When it is necessary for the line to be crossed at a place which is not a block post, the Crossing Keeper, before opening the gates, must satisfy himself that no approaching train is near ; he must then place his fixed signals, where provided, at Caution or Danger, as the case may be, and must not again lower them until the line is clear and the gates are closed across the roadway.

101. Where the gates on both sides of the line do not open simultaneously, the gate towards which the road traffic is approaching must not be opened until the opposite gate has been first opened. When, however, road traffic is approaching on both sides of the crossing the Crossing Keeper must use his discretion as to which gate should be first opened.

102. (a) Lamps on level crossing gates must, when

lighted, show a red light in each direction along the line when the gates are closed across it. The lamps must be lighted as soon as it commences to be dusk, and during fog or falling snow.

(b) On lines which are closed during the night, the lamps must be extinguished before the employee attending to the gates leaves duty, unless instructions are issued to the contrary or long burning lamps are provided. The lamps must, if necessary, be re-lighted for the passage of any train that may be run before daylight. When the line remains open during the night the lamps must not be extinguished until daylight.

103. Where hand or wicket gates are controlled from a signal box, the Signalman must operate the controlling arrangement when necessary to prevent persons crossing the line.

104. A Crossing Keeper must not, except as provided in Rule 197, clause (f), give any hand signal to the Driver of an approaching train if the line is clear. If, however, owing to an emergency, it is necessary to stop a train he must, unless he has means of advising the Signalman, place his fixed signals, where provided, to Caution or Danger, as the case may be, put down 3 detonators 10 yards apart, on the line or lines affected as far away as is necessary to ensure any train being brought to a stand clear of any obstruction, and exhibit a hand Danger signal. At level crossings where it is possible to communicate with the Signalman he must be informed of the circumstances, and, if

necessary, the foregoing provisions must also be carried out.

105. At level crossings which are not block posts, the fixed signals, where provided, must only be used for the protection of the crossing, or as prescribed in Rule 104.

106. The Crossing Keeper must satisfy himself that fixed signals, where provided, work properly. He must immediately report any defect in the signals, gates or other equipment to the Ganger, Lineman or other person in charge of repairs, and the matter must also be reported to the nearest Station Master.

107. (*a*) Unless special authority be given to the contrary, traction or other heavy engines, heavy vehicles or heavily-loaded vehicles, whether mechanically propelled or otherwise, or droves of animals, must not be allowed to cross the line when any train can be seen, or is known to be, approaching the crossing.

(*b*) Station Masters must, as far as practicable, request users of traction or other heavy engines in their neighbourhood to give reasonable notice to the nearest Station Master on each occasion of their intention to pass such engines over the line at a public level crossing not provided with fixed signals.

Station Masters must also request users of traction or other heavy engines, or heavy vehicles, whether mechanically propelled or otherwise, to give reasonable notice to the nearest Station Master on each occasion of their intention to pass such engines or vehicles over the line at an occupation level crossing.

(c) On receipt of the intimation referred to in clause (b), the Station Master must, except as otherwise provided in clause (d), arrange for a man with hand signals and detonators to be sent out at least ¾ mile from the level crossing in each direction, or to the nearest signal box if it is situated within that distance, to secure the safety of trains during the passage of the traction or other heavy engines, &c., across the line. If necessary the services of Lengthmen must be obtained for this purpose.

The same precautions must be taken by Station Masters in the case of other engines or vehicles should they be advised by the user that any such engine or vehicle is liable to be held up and so obstruct the line.

(d) Where telephonic communication is provided between the level crossing and the signal box, it will not be necessary to send out men as directed in clause (c), but the Crossing Keeper must communicate with the Signalman and obtain his permission for the traction or other heavy engine, &c., to cross the line. The Signalman must not give such permission after he has lowered his signals for, or has allowed, a train to proceed towards the crossing, nor when a train has been signalled to him from the box on the other side of the crossing, until he is satisfied that such train or trains have passed the crossing. After the Signalman has given permission for a traction or other heavy engine, &c., to cross the line he must not allow a train to proceed towards the crossing or give permission for a train to approach from the box on the other side of the crossing until he has ascertained from the Crossing Keeper that the traction or other heavy engine, &c., has passed over the line.

(e) In the event of any person after being advised in accordance with clause (b) crossing the line with a traction or other heavy engine at a public level crossing not provided with fixed signals, or with traction or other heavy engines, or heavy vehicles, whether mechanically propelled or otherwise, at an occupation level crossing, without giving notice to the nearest Station Master, the matter must be promptly reported to the **Divisional Superintendent of Operation, or in the case of the Northern Division the Operating Manager,** with the name and address of such person.

9

SAFE SHUNTING

Shunting is required when making up a train, adding or removing wagons en route, splitting it up at the end of a journey or placing a wagon in a better position for loading or unloading.

Although shunting is normally carried out by a locomotive, in the past horsepower or even manpower has been used to move single wagons either by pushing or using a pinch bar. At Newmarket, BR withdrew its last shunting horse in 1967.

Goods trains were often loose shunted, a locomotive propelling and then stopping, allowing an uncoupled vehicle to proceed under momentum. Fly shunting was employed to avoid a locomotive becoming trapped in a dead-end siding. An engine drew wagons along a line; wagons at the rear were detached on the move; the engine and the rest of the train then accelerated and the points quickly shifted to direct the following loose wagons to another siding. It was a dangerous procedure fraught with risks and only utilised if no other option was available.

Other methods for avoiding a locomotive becoming trapped were either to use a tow rope to move a wagon on an adjacent siding, or push a wagon by means of a timber prop placed between the engine and the last wagon. Sometimes gravity shunting was used. A train was propelled up a gradient and braked, the engine detached and run into a siding, after which the train was allowed to descend by gravity into another siding.

Shunting is a dangerous job as apart from wagons approaching almost silently, there may be obstacles such as point levers for the shunter to trip over and perhaps fall in front of a moving vehicle. One safety development was the shunter's pole, which came into general use in 1886 and obviated the need for men to pass between wagons when coupling, or uncoupling. In 1900 the Royal Commission on Accidents to Railway Servants found that the accident rate, of 5.08 fatalities per year per 1,000 employed, was even worse than that for miners. It recommended the provision of brake levers and destination labels on both sides of a wagon to avoid shunters continually having to cross the track and also recommended the abolition of tow-roping and propping. When fly-shunting a man often had to run alongside a wagon in order to apply the handbrake so that it did not strike other wagons in the siding too hard. The handbrake was given leverage with a brake stick.

SHUNTING.

108. During shunting operations Drivers must work only to signals given by the Guard, Shunter or other person in charge, and a Driver must not move his train until he has received such a signal although the fixed signal may have been lowered.

109. The person giving hand signals must do so in such a way as to avoid the signals being taken by any Driver other than the one for whom they are intended.

110. (a) Double shunting, i.e., the turning of some vehicles on to one line or siding and others on to another line or siding during one propelling movement, must only be carried out by experienced men.

When performing double shunting the men working

the points must see that the points are in the correct position for the movement, and Guards, Shunters, Signalmen and others concerned must have a clear understanding as to the points to be moved.

(*b*) Vehicles must not be loose shunted, *i.e.*, without remaining attached to the engine, into sidings or upon running lines unless, where necessary, they are accompanied a sufficient distance by a competent person prepared to apply the hand brakes, or sprags, to ensure the vehicles being brought to a stand at the required place, or to prevent them coming into violent contact with other vehicles, or the buffer stops, or fouling other lines.

Loose shunting of any vehicles, by engines, against loaded passenger vehicles, also loose shunting, by engines, of vehicles containing passengers or explosives is, however, strictly prohibited.

Loose shunting, by engines, of vehicles containing live stock should be avoided as far as possible, but may be adopted when absolutely necessary, provided the brake is in good order, and the Guard or Shunter controls the movement.

Loose shunting of vehicles into loading docks, stages, warehouse platforms, &c., is prohibited, unless the brakes can be applied without risk of injury to the men operating them.

(*c*) The movement of vehicles by means of a prop or pole, or by towing with a rope or chain attached to an engine or vehicle moving on an adjacent line, is prohibited, except where specially authorised by the **Chief Operating Manager.**

111. (*a*) Guards, Shunters and others engaged in shunting operations MUST SATISFY THEMSELVES that—

(i.) Trains or vehicles are clear of all points that require to be reversed.

(ii.) Vehicles placed in sidings are properly secured to prevent them from moving, fouling other lines, being blown out, or otherwise escaping on to a running line.

(iii.) After the operations are completed, trains or vehicles are left clear of any running lines and within trap points, derailers, or scotch blocks; that points not worked from a signal box are in their normal position; that scotch blocks, where provided, are placed across the rails; and that no vehicle is left inadvertently upon any running line.

(iv.) Where the movement is over hand points, that all points which become facing are in the correct position.

(v.) During frost or snow when there is a likelihood of points being prevented from closing, that all points which become facing points are properly closed before shunting movements are made over them.

(*b*) Where the movement is over points worked, bolted or locked from a signal box or ground frame, and a fixed signal is not provided for the movement, the Guard, Shunter or other person in charge must have an intimation verbally, or by hand signal or other authorised means, from the Signalman or person working the ground frame that the movement may be made, and must, as far as practicable, see that the points are in their correct position before giving a signal to the Driver to move.

(c) When an engine is unaccompanied by a Guard or Shunter, the Driver must carry out the provisions of clauses (a) and (b) of this Rule. He must also see that his train is clear after it has been set back into a refuge siding, through a crossover road or in any other similar case where the engine is near the points and there is not a Guard or Shunter present.

(d) Before any vehicle is shunted into a siding, the Guard, Shunter or other person in charge must ascertain the position of any vehicles in the siding, and signal the Driver accordingly so as to avoid undue impact with such vehicles or the buffer-stops.

(e) Vehicles standing in sidings must be properly secured and left sufficiently clear of the fouling points of any adjoining sidings or lines, to admit of anyone engaged in shunting operations passing safely between such vehicles and any vehicles that may be standing or are being shunted on adjoining sidings or lines.

112. (a) Before vehicles are moved in, or shunted into, a siding used for repairing vehicles or for loading or unloading traffic, or a goods shed or other building, where vehicles are already standing, Guards, Shunters, and others concerned must warn any employees or other persons who may be engaged in, about, or between the vehicles ; they must also request persons who may be loading or unloading not to remain in, or near to, vehicles which are likely to be moved by shunting operations, and must satisfy themselves that no road vehicle or animal is foul of any of the lines on

which shunting operations are about to be performed.

(*b*) Care must be taken to see that goods shed doors are open and all is clear before commencing shunting operations on shed lines, and that all doors of vehicles are properly secured by the fastenings provided for the purpose or are in such a position as will ensure that they will not come into contact with any obstruction when they are moved, care being also taken that the contents are not left in such a condition as would result in their falling from a vehicle when being moved.

113. Vehicles loaded with long timber or other long articles secured by chains or ropes and stanchions upon more than two wagons must not be shunted when a passenger train is passing or signalled to approach if the line on which the passenger train travels would be at all likely to become fouled should the wagons leave the rails. Guards, Shunters, Signalmen and others concerned must come to a proper understanding when necessary to stop the shunting of such vehicles.

114. (*a*) When vehicles are detached and left on any running line the Signalman must be at once informed in order that he may keep the necessary signals at Danger and take the proper steps for securing safety. Detached vehicles must be properly secured to prevent them moving, and at night and during fog or falling snow a red light must be shown at the rear of the vehicles, or, where necessary, at both front and rear, until they are placed in a siding or otherwise disposed of.

(*b*) The person in charge of the shunting must see that the necessary red light or lights are shown, and the Station Master must see that this is clearly under-stood by the men concerned. The Signalman must keep a good look-out and if he sees any vehicle has been detached from a train and left on any running line, he must take the necessary steps to protect it.

(c) When it is necessary for a train or vehicle to be placed outside a home signal this must not be done without the Signalman's permission, and, unless specially authorised, **no** train **without a brake van in rear** or vehicle **on which the brake cannot be firmly secured** must be placed outside a home signal where the line is on a falling gradient towards the signal box in rear.

115. (a) Vehicles must not be moved unless the doors are properly closed and fastened, except as provided in clause (b) of Rule 112.

(b) When vehicles have to be shunted into sidings on a rising gradient, the vehicles to be moved at one shunt must be limited to such a number as the engine can propel without travelling at excessive speed.

(c) When shunting at places on inclines van-brakes must be screwed down tightly, in addition to which sufficient hand-brakes must be securely applied, and sprags or hand-scotches used when necessary, to avoid the possibility of the train or any of the vehicles running down the incline. At such places sprags and hand-scotches must be kept ready for the purpose

116. (a) Vehicles must, when practicable, be attached to or detached from a passenger train without the train being moved.

(*b*) When vehicles are being moved by an engine for the purpose of being attached to, or detached from, a passenger train, the brake pipes, where provided, must be connected so that the continuous brake may be available during the operation.

Whenever it is necessary at stations where Absolute Block Working is in force, for an engine to be brought to the rear of a train for the purpose of attaching or detaching vehicles, or removing from the section vehicles which have been detached from a train which has gone forward, the operation must only be carried out after the Driver has been clearly verbally instructed by the person in charge what movement is to be made.

The Driver may, if necessary, be instructed to pass a signal at Danger for the purpose shown above.

(*c*) Before any vehicle containing passengers is moved over points, the person in charge of the operation must ascertain that the points are securely set, and that the line is clear and properly protected.

117. The standard code of audible signals by means of bell, gong, horn, whistle, or other appliance used for signalling to Drivers engaged in shunting operations is as follows :—

Signal.	Indicates.
One	Go ahead.
Two	Set back.
Three	Stop.
Four	Ease couplings.

118. Staff riding on engines or vehicles, or when on the ground alongside vehicles, at converging points in sidings must take special care that there is sufficient clearance for their safety.

SHUNTING AND COUPLING.

Employees must exercise proper care in getting between vehicles when coupling or uncoupling them and **shunting poles must be used** when practicable.

No attempt must be made to throw the link over the drawbar hook by means of a shunting pole until the buffers have actually touched.

Employees must not go **between vehicles or engines,** or between a vehicle and an engine, in any case where a gangway or gangways interpose, to couple or uncouple, **until the vehicle or engines are at rest.**

Employees must not remain between vehicles or engines, or between a vehicle and an engine, when a gangway or gangways interpose, during an "easing up" movement, but must stand clear of such vehicles or engines until they are at rest.

Employees must not go between coaching stock vehicles fitted with short buffers until the vehicles are at rest, or go between vehicles fitted with automatic couplings, except for the purpose of dealing with brake pipes or heating pipes, and this must **not be done until the vehicles are at rest.**

They must not go between two coaching stock vehicles without communicating gangways before they come together, except when this can be done with safety.

They must, whenever possible, couple goods wagons fitted with screw couplings by means of a shunting pole, and must not go between wagons in order to screw the couplings up until the vehicles are at rest.

When it is not possible to couple these vehicles by means of a shunting pole, employees must not go between the vehicles to couple up until they are at rest.

Goods wagons fitted with link couplings must be coupled or uncoupled with a shunting pole, and employees must not, except where absolutely necessary, go between the buffers. In cases where this cannot be avoided, they must wait until the wagons are at rest.

Double coupling of wagons.

When double coupling of wagons has to be resorted to, the vehicles must be at rest before being coupled or uncoupled (Rule 12).

Signals.

During shunting operations, Drivers must work only to signals given by the Guard, Shunter or other person in charge, and a Driver must not move his train until he has received such a signal although the fixed signal may have been lowered (Rule 108).

Movement of points.

During shunting operations, Signalmen must not move points until they have obtained a signal from the Guard or Shunter, or from the Driver or Fireman in the case of a light-engine, intimating that the last vehicle or the engine, as the case may be, is clear of the points. Guard or Shunter to give such signal at night or during fog or falling snow, by means of a *white* light moved quickly above the head. On the G.W.R. a *green* light held steadily at knee level must be used.

When a train has been set back into a refuge siding or through a cross-over road, or in any other similar case where the engine is near the points the signal will be given by the Driver.

After shunting operations are completed, the Signalman must see, or have intimation from the Guard, Shunter or Driver that the running lines are clear (Rule 69).

Loose shunting of any vehicles, by engines, against loaded passenger vehicles, also loose shunting, by engines, of vehicles containing **passengers or explosives** is, however, **strictly prohibited**; also vehicles containing live stock should be avoided as far as possible, but may be adopted when absolutely necessary, provided the brake is in good order, and the Guard or

Shunter **controls the movement.** Loose shunting of vehicles into loading docks, stages, warehouse platforms, etc., **is prohibited,** unless the brakes can be applied without risk of injury to the men operating them.

Propping, tow-roping and chaining.

The movement of vehicles by means of a prop or pole, or by towing with a rope or chain attached to an engine or vehicle moving on an adjacent line, **is prohibited,** except where specially authorised (Rule 110).

Vehicles to be clear of points.

Guards, Shunters and others engaged in shunting operations **must satisfy themselves** that—

Trains or vehicles are **clear of all points** that require to be reversed. Vehicles placed in sidings are **properly secured to prevent** them from moving, fouling other lines, being blown out, or otherwise escaping on to a running line. After the operations are completed, trains or vehicles are **left clear of any running lines** and within trap points, derailers or scotch blocks; that points not worked from a signal box are in their normal position; that scotch blocks, where provided are placed across the rails; and that no vehicle is left inadvertently upon any running line.

Where the movement is over hand points, that **all** points which become facing points are in the correct position, and during frost or snow when there is a likelihood of points being prevented from closing, that all points which become facing points are **properly closed** before shunting movements are made over them.

Shunting where no fixed signals exist.

Where the movement is over points worked, bolted or locked from a signal box or ground frame, and a fixed signal is not provided for the movement, the Guard, Shunter or other person in charge must have an intimation verbally, or by hand signal or other authorised means, from the Signalman or person working the ground frame that the movement may be made, and must, as far as practicable, see that the points are in their correct position before giving a signal to the Driver to move.

When an engine is unaccompanied by a Guard or Shunter the Driver must carry out the provisions of the clauses of this Rule. He must also see that his train is clear after it has been set back into a refuge siding, through a crossover road or in any other similar case where the engine is near the points and there is not a Guard or Shunter present.

Shunting into sidings.

Before any vehicle is shunted into a siding, the Guard, Shunter or other person in charge must ascertain the position of any vehicles in the siding, and signal the Driver accordingly so as to avoid undue impact with such vehicles or with the buffer-stops.

Vehicles standing in sidings.

Vehicles standing in sidings must be properly secured and left sufficiently clear of the fouling points of any adjoining sidings or lines (Rule 111).

Shunt sidings—Road vehicles to be clear.

Guards, Shunters and others concerned must warn any employees or other persons who may be engaged in, about, or between the vehicles; they must also request persons who may be loading or unloading not to remain in or near to, vehicles which are likely to be moved by shunting operations, and must satisfy themselves that no road vehicle or animal is foul of any of the lines on which shunting operations are about to be performed.

Shunting goods shed.

See that goods shed door is open and all is clear before commencing shunting, and that all doors of vehicles are properly secured or are in such a position as will ensure that they will not come into contact with any obstruction when they are moved, care being also taken that the contents are not left in such a condition as would result in their falling from a vehicle when being moved (Rule 112).

Vehicles loaded with long articles.

Vehicles loaded with long timber or other long articles secured by chains or ropes and stanchions upon more than two wagons **must not be shunted** when a passenger train is passing or signalled to approach if the line on which the passenger train travels would be at all likely to become fouled should the wagons leave the rails (Rule 113).

Vehicles—Doors to be closed.

Vehicles must not be moved unless the doors are properly closed and fastened, except as provided in Rule 112.

Sidings on rising gradients.

When vehicles have to be shunted into sidings on a rising gradient, the vehicles to be moved at one shunt must be limited to such a number as the engine can propel without travelling at excessive speed.

When shunting at places on inclines, van-brakes must be screwed down tightly, in addition to which sufficient hand brakes must be securely applied, and sprags or hand-scotches used when necessary, to avoid the possibility of the train or any of the vehicles running down the incline. At such places sprags and hand-scotches must be kept ready for the purpose (Rule 115).

Attaching and detaching.

Vehicles must, when practicable, be attached to or detached from a passenger train without the train being moved. When vehicles are being moved by an engine for the purpose of being attached to or detached from, a passenger train, the brake pipes, where provided, must be connected so that the continuous brake may be available during the operation.

L.M.S.R. addition.—

Whenever it is necessary at stations where absolute block working is in force for an engine to be brought to the rear of a train for the purpose of attaching or detaching vehicles, or removing from the section vehicles which have been detached from a train which has gone forward, the operation must only be carried out after the Driver has been clearly verbally instructed by the person in charge what movement is to be made.

The Driver may, if necessary, be instructed to pass a signal at Danger for the purpose shewn above.

Passenger trains over points.

Before any vehicle containing passengers is moved over points, the person in charge of the operation must ascertain that the points are **securely set,** and that the line is clear and properly protected (Rule 116).

Code of audible signals.

The standard code of audible signals by means of bell, gong, horn, whistle, or other appliances used for signalling to Drivers engaged in shunting operations is as follows (Rule 117)

SIGNAL	INDICATES
One ....Go ahead
Two ....Set back.
Three ....Stop.
Four ....Ease couplings.

10

HEAD, TAIL & SIDE LAMPS

Headlamps are necessary to give warning of a train's approach either at night, or in a tunnel, while a tail lamp is necessary to protect a train's rear and also form a check that a train is complete. A signalman was required to see that a train carried a tail lamp, because if it did not, part of that train could still be in the section to the rear. Oil lamps were used as they had been found generally reliable.

By the 1880s headlamps indicated the class of train – goods or passenger, fast or slow – but many railways in the South indicated route rather than class.

HEAD, TAIL AND SIDE LAMPS.

119. Each engine, or leading engine when two or more engines are coupled together, and each rail motor, motor train, or electric train, must carry the prescribed head lamps, discs, or indicators, and destination boards where provided. The head lamps and indicators must be alight after sunset and during fog or falling snow, and where otherwise provided.

120. (a) Each train when on any running line must always have a tail lamp, properly cleaned and trimmed, attached to the rear of the last vehicle, and this lamp will furnish evidence to the Signalman and others that the train is complete. After sunset, or during fog or falling snow, or when the block apparatus has failed in a section where there is a tunnel, or where otherwise provided, the tail lamp must be alight and show a red light and, except in the case of passenger and other trains composed of coaching stock, and light engines, two red side lights must also be carried.

(b) The Guard, if there be only one, or rear Guard if there be more than one, must see that the tail lamps, and side lamps where provided, are kept properly burning when necessary.

121. Where trains travel in the same direction on parallel lines, special regulations for head, side and tail lamps will be issued as necessary.

122. (*a*) An engine without a train must, when on any running line, always carry a tail lamp in the rear.

(*b*) When two or more engines are run coupled together without a train, the last engine only must have a tail lamp attached.

(*c*) An engine or engines drawing a train must not carry any lamp in the rear.

(*d*) An engine assisting a train in the rear must have a tail lamp attached ; when more than one engine assists, the tail lamp must be carried on the rearmost engine only.

123. Engines employed exclusively in shunting at station yards and sidings must, after sunset or during fog or falling snow, carry head and tail lamps both showing a red light or such other light as may be prescribed.

124. (*a*) An additional tail lamp or a red board or a red flag by day, or an additional red tail light by night, carried on the last vehicle of a train or on any engine, indicates that a special train is to follow, of which previous printed or written notice has not been given. Signalmen and others concerned must keep a look out for such indication.

(*b*) The Station Master at the starting point of any such special train must, when practicable, take care that the additional tail signal is affixed on the last vehicle of the preceding train and the Guard must see that the additional tail signal is removed when no longer required.

125. (*a*) When slip carriages are run on a train the indications must be as follow :—

On the rear of the slip portion when there is only one such portion.
On the rear of the last portion to be slipped when there is more than one slip portion.

On the rear of the first portion to be slipped when there are two slip portions.
On the rear of the second portion to be slipped when there are three slip portions.

On the rear of the first portion to be slipped when there are three slip portions.

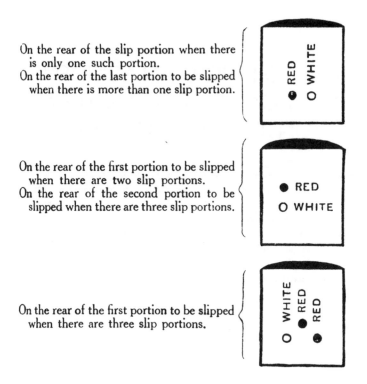

By day the lamps must be encircled by discs of the same colour as the lights shown by night.

(*b*) A white head light must be carried on the leading end of each portion to be slipped after sunset and during fog or falling snow.

11

HOW TO REPORT AN ACCIDENT & ACTION TO BE TAKEN AT AN UNTOWARD STOPPAGE

Although railways are a very safe method of transport if the rules are obeyed, there is always the chance of accident and because a railway accident is such a rare thing, it receives undue publicity from the press.

In the early days boiler explosions were not infrequent, sometimes due to thin boiler plates and sometimes due to safety valves being screwed down to give a higher steam pressure. For instance in June 1849 0-6-0 *Goliah* (an alternative spelling of 'Goliath') was approaching the foot of Hemerdon incline on the South Devon Railway when its firebox crown collapsed. Fortunately the footplate crew were not killed. When the Board of Trade inspector tested the safety valves he discovered that they lifted at 150 lb per square inch instead of at the locomotive's working pressure of 70 lb.

In 1850 a London & North Western Railway locomotive exploded at Wolverton. The engine, standing in the yard, had been blowing off steam for some time and a labourer who found the sound annoying stopped it by screwing down the safety valves. The engine retaliated by slicing off one of his unduly sensitive ears with a flying fragment.

Sometimes accidents were caused through passengers' inexperience with the new form of transport – an example being William Huskisson standing on the track and getting run over and killed at the opening of the Liverpool & Manchester Railway.

In medieval times anything which caused the death of a person was required to be forfeited to the Crown and was known as a deodand. Thus if a steam engine caused a fatal accident, it became a deodand.

For example, on 24 December 1841 a Down GWR goods train consisted of the broad gauge 2-4-0 *Hecla,* two third-class coaches, a parcels van and seventeen goods wagons. In the darkness, *Hecla* plunged into a slip which had occurred on the Down line. This sudden stop caused the weight of the goods wagons to crush the two third-class coaches against the engine and tender, causing the death of eight passengers and injury to seventeen. At the inquest on the victims, the jury laid a deodand of £1,000 on *Hecla* and her train. Lt-Col. Sir Frederick Smith's report exonerated the GWR from blame and the company appealed successfully against the claim which was reduced to a nominal sum. Deodands were abolished in 1846.

As courts and coroners' juries were unable to understand the technical side of railways, it was believed that the government should undertake the role of safety, so the Regulation of Railways Act of 1840 obliged railway companies to report to the Board of Trade all accidents causing injury. The 1842 Regulation of Railways Act restricted this requirement to serious accidents only, 'whether attended with personal injury or not'. The Board of Trade inspectors were officers drawn from the Corps of the Royal Engineers, Lt-Col. Sir Frederick Smith being appointed the first Inspector General of Railways.

Many of the railway accidents of the nineteenth century were caused either by inadequate signalling – such as the use of the time interval system controlling the separation of trains, rather than the block system where a line was divided into sections – or by the lack of continuous brakes. A few were caused by construction problems, such as the fall of the Tay Bridge on 28 December1879.

In its original design this bridge, almost 2 miles in length, was of lattice girders supported on brick piers. In the event, it was discovered that the bed of the Tay was not as solid as expected and it was decided to substitute cast iron columns which would be lighter. The bridge, then the longest in the world, was completed in 1878.

On 28 December a gale was so fierce that, after delivering the single line staff to the driver, the signalman had to crawl back to his box on all fours. He watched the departing train, saw a flash of light and then darkness. All thirteen of the main girders had been unable to withstand the increased pressure of the gale on the surface of the train, so both spans and train collapsed into the water. The disaster was caused by the failure of the bracing ties and the cast iron lugs to which they were secured.

Only rarely did a mechanical failure cause a railway accident. On 24 December 1874 a Down train left Oxford and a quarter of a mile south of a bridge over the Oxford Canal a small portion of a tyre on the small leading coach became detached.

Driver Richard, glancing back, observed snow and ballast flying up. Concerned, he sounded his deep-toned brake whistle, but before the guards had time to respond to his signal, Driver Richards and the driver of the pilot engine had shut off steam, reversed and applied their brakes while the firemen were screwing down the tender brakes.

This action meant that the pull of the couplings ceased to hold the small leading coach in line and the momentum of the train crushed it to matchwood. Nine coaches fell over the bridge into the canal, killing thirty-four passengers and injuring sixty-five.

Very occasionally locomotive design was at fault. An example of this was the Sevenoaks derailment on 24 August 1927. Tank engines were particularly suitable for relatively short journeys; they also offered the advantage of better travelling conditions when in reverse, giving protection from the wind and coal dust, combined with better visibility.

River Class 2-6-4T No. 800 *River Cray* headed the 5.00 p.m. Cannon Street to Folkestone express. About midway between Dunton Green and Sevenoaks, Driver Buss heard a knocking (which proved to be the wheel flanges striking the chairs), closed the regulator and then applied the brake At a speed of approximately 60 mph the engine dipped and lurched because the pony truck was off the road. This pair of wheels continued to travel close to and parallel with the rails for about 500 yards until it reached trailing catch points, which it burst open, derailing the locomotive and train.

As the line was in a shallow cutting, the derailment might not have been serious but for the fact that an overbridge had separate arches for Up and Down lines. The engine and first two coaches passed safely through, but the others were damaged by the bridge piers. Thirteen passengers were killed and twenty-one seriously injured.

When an engine of the same class was tested on the excellent permanent way of the former Great Northern Railway between St Neots and Huntingdon, the engine rode steadily and it was decided that the trouble lay with the rather less than ideal Southern Railway track. When an irregular depression in the road coincided with the roll of an engine, a dangerous condition arose. The poor SR track also affected riding of the coaches and one passenger reported that when he washed his hands, most of the water shot out of the basin on to the floor.

It was considered not so likely that such irregularities would occur as close to each other as to coincide with the shorter rolling periods of tender engines, so the outcome was that the 2-6-4Ts were converted to 2-6-0s and the SR permanent way improved.

REPORTING OF ACCIDENTS.

177.   All accidents or obstructions must be promptly reported to the Chief and District Officers concerned, an advice being sent by speaking instrument in the case of serious mishaps.

In case of personal injury, the names and addresses of witnesses must be obtained.

When an accident to a train, or an obstruction, or a failure of any part of the works affecting the safety of the line, occurs, the next station or signal box open on each side must be immediately communicated with by the most expeditious means to enable Drivers and Guards of approaching trains to be advised of the circumstances, and assistance to be obtained if necessary.   In addition to advising the Chief and District Officers concerned, the Controller, and District Traffic Inspector must be immediately advised ; also if necessary, the Permanent-way Inspector, the locomotive depot where the breakdown vans for the district are kept, **the Carriage and Wagon District Foreman,** and the Signal and Telegraph Inspectors must be at once informed.

The stations where the starting of other trains is liable to be affected by delay caused by the accident or obstruction must be immediately advised.

TRAINS STOPPED BY ACCIDENT, FAILURE, OBSTRUCTION OR OTHER EXCEPTIONAL CAUSE.

178. (*a*) Should a train be stopped by accident, failure, obstruction or other exceptional cause the Guard or Guards, and the Fireman, must at once ascertain if any other line or lines used by trains running in the opposite or in the same direction are also obstructed, and, if so, they must immediately protect the obstruction on those lines in accordance with Rule 180. Where it is necessary for the Guard and Fireman to proceed towards each other for the purpose of ascertaining whether the opposite line is obstructed they must proceed along the off side (right-hand side in the running direction) of their train wherever practicable.

Immediately the train comes to a stand the Fireman unless he is aware that a line in the opposite direction is obstructed, must proceed along the off side (right-hand side in the running direction) of his train wherever practicable, to the Guard and convey to him the Driver's request for any assistance that may be required. The Guard must also proceed along the same side of the train towards the Fireman to confer with him, and must then protect the train in the rear in accordance with Rule 179, except that should the Guard have been advised or be aware that the block apparatus has failed he must, after satisfying himself that no line used by trains running in the opposite or in the same direction is obstructed, at once go back and protect his train.

In the case of a single line of railway if assistance is not required and the train is not foul of, or dangerously near to, any adjoining line, it will not be necessary for the train to be protected in accordance with Rule 179, provided that on the train coming to a stand the Driver shows the Guard, or Fireman in the case of a light engine, the train staff or electric token, or when working by Pilotman is in operation on such single line of railway the train is accompanied by the Pilotman.

(*b*) Should the train have arrived at the home signal or any line be obstructed within the protection of home signals worked from a signal box, the Guard or Fireman nearest to the box, must immediately advise the Signalman of the circumstances, and if no train is approaching on the obstructed line or lines, the instructions contained in Rules 179, 180 and 181 need not be carried out, except when the block apparatus has failed and (i.) the train is standing at the home signal, (ii.) the whole of it is not within the protection of that signal, (iii.) the train has arrived within the home signal and that signal remains in the Clear position. In all cases, however, should a train be approaching on the obstructed line or lines, the Guard or Fireman must immediately go toward such train exhibiting a hand Danger signal and put down detonators in accordance with Rules 179, 180 and 181 in addition to advising the Signalman.

(*c*) Should a train be detained at a station by station duties for a period of five minutes beyond its booked time and the signal box is switched out of circuit, the Station Master will be held responsible for the signals being placed at Danger, where the train can be protected by such means, except as shown in the last paragraph of this clause. The signals must again be lowered after the train has left the station and is continuing its journey. At places where fixed signal protection cannot be afforded, the Station Master must arrange for the Guard, or some other competent person, to protect the train in accordance with Rule 179 and must see that the necessary detonators, flag, and hand lamp are readily available to enable these instructions to be complied with. At places where there is no station staff on duty the Fireman must protect the train.

Where possible, the Signalmen at the box in advance and at the box in rear must be advised that the train is so detained.

The fixed signals must not be relied upon for the protection of a train unless they are plainly visible to the Driver of an approaching train, and the signal lamps are lighted, if necessary.

Where the signals are interlocked with the block instruments the signals must not be placed at Danger for the protection of the train, but the train must be protected in accordance with Rule 179.

(d) In the case of electric trains, the Motorman, where no Assistant Motorman is employed, must carry out the duties of the Fireman.

179. (a) Should the train not foul or not be dangerously near to any other line, the Guard if there be only one, or the rear Guard if there be more than one, must go back not less than $\frac{3}{4}$-mile, unless he

arrive at a signal box within that distance, exhibiting a hand Danger signal to stop any train approaching on the obstructed line, and he must place detonators upon one rail of the obstructed line, as under, viz. :—

1 Detonator $\frac{1}{4}$-mile from his train,

1 Detonator $\frac{1}{2}$-mile from his train, and

3 Detonators, 10 yards apart, not less than $\frac{3}{4}$-mile from his train.

Should a train approach on the obstructed line before the detonators have been laid down as prescribed, the Guard must immediately place 3 detonators on the line affected, as far as possible from the obstruction, and exhibit a hand Danger signal.

(b) In order to secure as quickly as possible the safety of the line and to obtain assistance and to regulate the working of the traffic, the Guard, after protecting his train by detonators, as above directed, must go to the signal box in rear, except as otherwise provided in the following paragraph and clause (f) of this Rule, continuing to exhibit a hand Danger signal, and advise the Signalman of the circumstances.

If it is not necessary for the Guard to go to the signal box in rear he must, except as provided in Rule 181 (c) and Rule 183 (c), remain at the $\frac{3}{4}$-mile point exhibiting a hand Danger signal to stop any train approaching on the obstructed line, until recalled by the Driver sounding the engine whistle or by other means. Should he be recalled either before or after reaching the prescribed distance he must leave on the rail at the point from which he is recalled 3 detonators, 10 yards apart, and return to his train, taking up on the way any other detonators he may have put down.

(c) Should assistance be obtained from the signal box in rear, the Guard must ride on the engine of the assisting train, and indicate to the Driver the position of the disabled train.

The assisting train must run at reduced speed, and great caution must be observed by all concerned.

(d) Except as provided in the following paragraph it will not be necessary for the Signalman concerned to detain the assisting train until the arrival of the Guard of the disabled train at the signal box, automatic stop signal or semi-automatic stop signal working automatically in rear of the disabled train, if information has been received that the Guard is coming back. On receipt of this information the Signalman concerned may allow the assisting train to enter the obstructed section after the Driver has been informed of the circumstances and instructed to keep a good look-out for the Guard. If there is a tunnel in the obstructed section the Driver of the assisting train must not enter such tunnel unless the Guard of the disabled train has come back and met the train, or it has been ascertained that the tunnel is clear and that the Guard is not in the tunnel.

On double lines of railway during fog or falling snow, the assisting train must be detained at the signal box, automatic stop signal or semi-automatic stop signal working automatically in rear of the disabled train until the Guard of the disabled train has arrived thereat, when he must so advise the Signalman.

(*e*) Should the engine obtained from the rear have to return in the wrong direction, the prescribed " Wrong Line " order, in accordance with Rule 184, should be obtained from the Signalman before the assisting engine enters the obstructed section.

(*f*) If the signal box in advance of the obstruction is nearer, or could be more quickly reached, then in order to advise the Signalmen concerned of the cause of the obstruction, and to arrange for assistance, the engine, if it be able to run forward, must be detached, and the Driver must proceed to the signal box in advance, having, if necessary, first obtained from the Guard protecting the train an order to return in the wrong direction as provided for in Rule 183 (*f*).   If the engine cannot be used for the purpose, the Fireman must go forward to the signal box and advise the Signalman of the circumstances, and, if it has been decided to obtain assistance from the front, and it is necessary for an assisting engine or breakdown van train to travel in the wrong direction to the disabled train, the Fireman must take with him a " Wrong Line " order from the Driver as provided for in Rule 183 (*g*).

If when the Fireman arrives at the signal box in advance it be found that assistance is not available at that point, but can be given from the rear, the Fireman must at once return with the " Wrong Line " order to the Driver, who must cancel the order (by writing the word " Cancelled " across it, and the time of cancellation), and send the Fireman back with the cancelled order to advise the Guard that assistance will be given from the rear instead of from the front. The Signalman at the signal box in advance must immediately advise the Signalman at the signal box in rear of the circumstances, and request that an assisting train be sent in from the rear ; the assisting train may then, except during fog or falling snow, be allowed to enter the obstructed section in accordance with clause (d) of this Rule. The Guard protecting the disabled train, must stop the assisting train and not allow it to proceed to the rear of the disabled train until he has been advised by the Fireman of the altered arrangements for rendering assistance, and has seen the Driver's cancelled " Wrong Line " order, which the Fireman must afterwards return to the Driver.

During fog or falling snow it will be necessary for the Guard, after seeing the Driver's cancelled " Wrong Line " order, to proceed as quickly as possible to the signal box in rear, and accompany the assisting train.

(g) In the case of electric trains, the Motorman, where no Assistant Motorman is employed, must carry out the duties of the Fireman.

(h) When it is necessary for a Motorman to issue a " Wrong Line " order, he must himself (if an Assistant Motorman is not employed) go forward and deliver it to the Signalman at the box in advance.

(i) Should, for any reason, there be no Guard or the services of the Guard not be available, or should the stoppage or failure occur to a light engine, the Fireman must carry out the duties of the Guard.

(*j*) When a train is brought to a stand in a section in advance of an automatic or semi-automatic stop signal, the provisions of this Rule must be carried out, except that it will be necessary for the Guard to go back a distance of only ¼-mile, or to the first stop signal in rear of his train if such signal is within that distance, and to protect his train by placing on the rail 3 detonators, 10 yards apart, at that point. If the Guard in going back finds that the first stop signal in rear of his train is not at Danger he must place one detonator on the rail at the signal, proceed for a further distance of ¼-mile and there protect his train with 3 detonators.

If assistance is required from the rear and the disabled train is at a stand more than ¼-mile ahead of the stop signal the Guard after protecting his train as directed above must continue to proceed towards that stop signal and carry out the provisions of clause (*c*).

180. (*a*) Should the train foul, or be dangerously near to, any line or lines used by trains running in the opposite direction, in addition to the Guard going back to protect the train in accordance with Rule 179 or clause (*b*) of this Rule, the Driver of the disabled train must immediately detach his engine, if it be able to travel, and run forward with it not less than ¾-mile from the obstruction, where the Fireman must place 3 detonators, 10 yards apart, on any obstructed line or lines used by trains running in the opposite direction, and rejoin his engine.

In running forward the Driver must sound the engine whistle, exhibit a hand Danger signal, and, in addition, show a red head light when passing through a tunnel, or after sunset or during fog or falling snow, in order to stop any train that may be approaching on the opposite line or lines. Should a train approach on the obstructed line or lines before the detonators have been laid down as prescribed, the Fireman must immediately place 3 detonators on the line or lines affected as far as possible from the obstruction.

After the detonators have been put down, the Driver must continue to go forward with his engine to the nearest signal box, sounding the engine whistle, and inform the Signalman of the circumstances.

Should the engine be disabled or there be any delay in detaching it, the Fireman must at once go forward, exhibiting a hand Danger signal, and place detonators on any obstructed line or lines used by trains running in the opposite direction, as under, viz. :—

    1 Detonator $\frac{1}{4}$-mile from the obstruction,
    1 Detonator $\frac{1}{2}$-mile from the obstruction, and
    3 Detonators, 10 yards apart, not less• than $\frac{3}{4}$-mile from the obstruction.

Should a train approach on the obstructed line or lines, before the detonators have been laid down as prescribed, the Fireman must immediately place 3 detonators on the line or lines affected, as far as possible from the obstruction, and exhibit a hand Danger signal.

After the detonators have been put down, the Fireman must continue to go forward to the nearest signal box, exhibiting a hand Danger signal, and inform the Signalman of the circumstances. Should the services of a Fireman not be available, as in the case of an electric train or for any other reason, the Driver must perform the duties of the Fireman.

(b) Should the train foul, or be dangerously near to, any adjoining line or lines on which trains travel in the same direction, the Guard must (if he is aware that the Enginemen are available to protect the opposite line if necessary) immediately protect such adjoining line or lines as well as the line on which his train was running, in the manner described in Rule 179.

In such case after the Guard has protected the obstruction in the rear on the line or lines affected, he must, if any line or lines used by trains running in the opposite direction have been obstructed, satisfy himself that they are protected in accordance with clause (a) of this Rule.

(c) Should the train foul, or be dangerously near to, any line or lines used by trains running in the same or opposite direction, and the services of a Guard not be available, the Driver must immediately send his Fireman forward to act in accordance with clause (a) of this Rule, and must himself go back or send some other competent person to protect the obstruction in the rear in accordance with Rule 179 and, if necessary, clause (b) of this Rule, so that the obstruction may be protected in both directions. Should the services of a Fireman also not be available, the Driver must arrange, if possible, for some competent person to protect the obstruction in the rear in accordance with Rule 179 and, if necessary, clause (b) of this Rule, and go forward himself and protect the line or lines used by trains running in the opposite direction as laid down in clause (*a*) of this Rule.

Should no competent person be available the Driver must, after protecting the obstructed line or lines used by trains running in the opposite direction, immediately return and protect the rear of his train as laid down in Rule 179 and, if necessary, clause (*b*) of this Rule. Should, however, an adjoining line or lines used by trains running in the same direction be also obstructed he must use his discretion as to which line he protects first, but must protect all obstructed lines with as little delay as possible.

(*d*) Should the train foul, or be dangerously near to, any line or lines used by trains running in the same or opposite direction, and the Driver run forward without being aware of the accident, or should for any reason the services of the Enginemen not be available, the Guard must arrange, if possible, for some competent person to protect the obstruction in the rear, in accordance with Rule 179 and, if necessary, clause (*b*) of this Rule, and go forward himself and protect the line or lines used by trains running in the opposite direction as laid down in clause (*a*) of this Rule.

Should no competent person be available the Guard must act in accordance with the instructions laid down for the Driver in the last paragraph of clause (*c*) of this Rule.

(*e*) If an assisting train or breakdown van train is required to enter the obstructed section, arrangements must be made in accordance with Rule 179, clauses (*c*), (*d*) and (*e*), or clause (*f*) as the case may be.

181. (a) Should the Guard, Driver or Fireman, as the case may be, in carrying out the instructions in Rule 179 (a) or (b), or 180 (a), (b), (c) or (d), or clause (f) of this Rule arrive at a signal box within or beyond the ¾-mile point from the obstruction, he must place 3 detonators, 10 yards apart, on the obstructed line or lines in such a position as to prevent any train entering the obstructed section without passing over the detonators, and inform the Signalman of the circumstances. The Signalman receiving this information must place or maintain the necessary signals at Danger to protect the obstructed line or lines and advise the Signalman at the box at the other end of the section of the circumstances.

The man who has gone to the rear box in accordance with Rule 179 (a) or (b), or 180 (b), (c) or (d) must, after carrying out the above instructions, either return to his train, or wait to accompany an assisting train according to circumstances.

The man who has gone to the box in advance in accordance with Rule 180 (a) must, after carrying out the above instructions, act under the instructions of the Station Master or Signalman, as the case may be.

Should the man in carrying out the instructions contained in Rule 180 (c) or (d) arrive at a signal box in advance or in rear, he must at once return and protect his train in the other direction, unless he is satisfied that this is being done in which case he must act under the instructions of the Station Master or Signalman, as the case may be.

The 3 detonators placed on the obstructed line or lines at a signal box must not be taken up until intimation has been received that the obstruction has been removed. Should the detonators be exploded, they must be replaced by the Signalman.

(*b*) The Signalman receiving information of the obstruction from the Signalman at the other end of the section must place or maintain the necessary signals at Danger to protect the obstructed line or lines, and place 3 detonators on the line as prescribed in clause (*a*) until the obstruction has been removed. Should the detonators be exploded they must be replaced by the Signalman.

(*c*) Should the distance prescribed in Rules 179 (*a*) or (*j*) and 180 (*a*) fall within a tunnel, or close to the mouth of a tunnel nearer to the obstruction, or in any other position where, owing to the formation of the line or to some other circumstance, the Driver of an approaching train would be unable to obtain a good and distant view of the hand Danger signal, the signal must be exhibited and detonators placed on the line at the end of the tunnel farther from the obstruction, or at such a distance over and above the prescribed distance as may be necessary to ensure the Driver obtaining a good and distant view of such signal.

Before entering any tunnel the man must place 3 detonators on the line, 10 yards apart, at the end of the tunnel nearer to the obstruction.

(*d*) After the obstruction has been removed the next train to pass through the section on each line affected must be stopped, the Driver advised of the circumstances, and instructed to travel cautiously through the section.

(*e*) Should a train, assisted by an engine in rear, be stopped by accident, failure, obstruction or other exceptional cause, and no other line or lines be obstructed, the protection of the train must be carried out by the Guard. Should any other line or lines be obstructed the services of the Fireman of the assisting engine must be utilised as necessary.

(*f*) In the case of a passenger train being stopped by the use of the communication between passenger, Guard, and Driver, the Fireman must, if there be only one Guard, go back and protect the train whilst the Guard attends to the requirements of the passenger who used the communication. Should there be two Guards the rear Guard must go back and protect the train whilst the front Guard attends to the requirements of the passenger. Should there be no Guard, the Fireman must go back and protect the train whilst the Driver attends to the passenger.

(*g*) Should the Guard, Driver or Fireman, as the case may be, when proceeding to the signal box after placing detonators on the obstructed line or lines in accordance with Rules 179 (*b*) or 180 (*a*), (*b*), (*c*) or (*d*), arrive at a station or other point where telephone communication exists which would enable earlier intimation to be given to the Signalman in regard to the obstruction and as to whether assistance is required, this must be used ; the Guard, Driver or Fireman must afterwards proceed to the signal box if necessary.

(*h*) In the case of electric trains, the Motorman,

where no assistant Motorman is employed, must carry out the duties of the Fireman.

(*i*) In the case of a propelled train, should the train foul, or be dangerously near to, any line or lines used by trains running in the opposite or same direction, the Guard must at once go forward and carry out the duties of the Fireman and the Fireman must at once go back and carry out the duties of the Guard as prescribed in Rule 180.

182. A Driver, on seeing a green hand signal waved slowly from side to side from a signal box, must understand that his train is divided, exercise great caution and look out for the rear portion. The green hand signal waved slowly from side to side is also the authority for the Driver to pass the signal controlling the entrance to the section ahead worked from the box at which the green hand signal is exhibited should that signal be at Danger, but when doing so he must understand that the line ahead is not necessarily clear and that he has been allowed to enter the section for the purpose of avoiding or reducing the force of a collision with the rear portion and must keep a good look-out ahead.

The green hand signal must not be exhibited unless it is intended that the front portion of the divided train should enter the section in advance.

183. (*a*) When a train or portion of a train is left on any running line from accident or inability of the engine to take the whole forward, or from any other cause, the Driver must not return for it on the same

line, except as ordered in clauses (*f*) and (*g*) of this Rule, but must cross on to, and travel along, the proper line, and must re-cross at the nearest point behind the part left, which he must push before him until convenient to go in front again with the engine. If there be a crossover road immediately in front of the train, and the operation can be performed within sight of the Signalman, the Driver may use such crossover road for the purpose of attaching his engine in front of the train.

(*b*) In cases where it is necessary to divide a goods train on an incline, owing to the inability of the engine to take the whole forward, both portions must, where practicable, be worked up the incline with a brake van in the rear. When a train is divided in this way at a station, or at an intermediate signal box, where a portion of the train can be disposed of, it will generally be found most convenient to shunt the front portion of the train into a siding, and take the rear portion forward first (with the brake van attached in rear) to the next station or signal box where there are means of disposing of it.

After the first portion of the train has been disposed of, the engine must return on the proper line, with the brake van, for the purpose of working forward the other portion of the train which has been left behind, and the brake van must, in that case also, be attached in the rear.

(*c*) Where a train is divided in a section between two signal boxes a tail lamp must not be carried on the engine or last vehicle of the front portion of the train before reaching the signal box in advance, where the Driver must stop and inform the Signalman of the circumstances ; if the engine or front portion of the train has to pass into the next section a tail lamp must then be placed in the rear. The Signalman must not give the " Train out of section " signal until he has satisfied himself that the whole of the train has arrived.

After sunset, or during fog or falling snow, or if the division is made in a tunnel, the man who divides the train must place 3 detonators, 10 yards apart, on the line not less than 100 yards ahead of the portion left behind.

In the case of the train being accidentally divided the Guard in charge after protecting the rear portion must then return and place 3 detonators, 10 yards apart, on the line not less than 100 yards ahead of the portion left behind, afterwards taking the most expeditious steps to obtain assistance.

A white light must be placed on the leading vehicle of the rear portion before that portion is propelled to the signal box in advance or drawn back to the signal box in rear.

(d) When two Guards are employed with a train which has to be divided in a section the Guard in charge, after putting on the rear brake and securing the rear portion of the train so that it will remain stationary, must go back and protect it in accordance with Rule 179. The other Guard must uncouple the train, and ride on the front portion.

When there is only one Guard with the train, the Fireman must uncouple and ride upon the front portion, and the Guard must take the necessary measures to protect the rear portion.

The Guard or Fireman travelling with the front portion must ride upon the last vehicle or the nearest suitable vehicle thereto. If there is no suitable vehicle he may ride on the engine.

(e) If the last vehicle of the front portion is not suitable for the Guard or Fireman to ride upon in accordance with clause (d), the Guard or Fireman must, before leaving with the front portion take such steps as will enable him to be in a position to assure the Signalman on arrival at the box in advance that the front portion of the train has arrived complete.

(f) If it be found necessary to return to the train or rear portion of the train in the wrong direction from the signal box in advance, the Driver must send his Fireman to the Guard to obtain his written authority to the Signalman at the first signal box in advance, authorising him to allow the engine to return from that point in the wrong direction (see Form A at end of Rule) and without this authority the Signalman must not allow the engine to return in the wrong direction to its train. The Signalman must retain this order. After giving such authority the Guard must continue to protect his train in the rear.

If the train, or rear portion of the train, has been left a short distance ahead of a signal box and is standing in such a position that the engine returning for it in the wrong direction will have to pass over any points worked from that signal box, the Guard, before issuing the " Wrong Line " order, must have it countersigned by the Signalman.

In the event of an engine assisting the train in the rear, the Guard's " Wrong Line " order must be countersigned by the Driver of that engine.

If the front portion of the train cannot be disposed of at the first signal box in advance, and it is necessary for the engine and front portion of the train to proceed to a signal box further ahead, the Driver must, if there is no crossover road at the first signal box, obtain from the Signalman there, before proceeding, a " Wrong Line " order (Form D—*see* Rule 184) to return in the wrong direction from the box in advance. If, however, there is a crossover road at the first signal box the engine must be returned on the proper line of rails to that signal box and be there crossed to the line on which the rear portion of the train is standing, so that the engine shall not travel in the wrong direction further than is absolutely necessary.

A " Wrong Line " order form must be issued for each occasion on which it is necessary for the engine to return in the wrong direction, as described above.

In the event of a train or portion of a train being left on a running line after the engine has been detached and removed from the line, and it is necessary for an engine to remove the train or for a breakdown van train to travel in the wrong direction from the signal box in advance, the Guard must issue a " Wrong Line " order (Form A) which must be conveyed to the Signalman at the first signal box in advance and the provisions of this Rule must be observed so far as they apply.

(*g*) When a train is brought to a stand on any running line, owing to the failure of the engine or from any other exceptional cause, it may be necessary for the engine coming to the assistance of the train or for the breakdown van train to travel in the wrong direction from the signal box in advance. In such a case the Driver of the disabled train must write out an authority on Form B (*see* end of Rule), for the Signalman at the first signal box in advance to allow the assisting engine, or the breakdown van train to travel in the wrong direction to the disabled train. The Fireman of the disabled train must hand the written authority to the Signalman, and accompany the assisting engine, or the breakdown van train, to his train, advising the Driver where, and under what circumstances, the disabled train is situated; the Signalman must retain the authority and show it to the Driver before allowing the assisting engine or breakdown van train to proceed in the wrong direction. The Driver of the disabled train after giving the order for the assisting engine or the breakdown van train to travel in the wrong direction, must not allow his train to be moved until the assisting engine or the breakdown van train arrives, unless satisfactory arrangements have been previously made to prevent the assisting engine or breakdown van train from coming in the wrong direction, and his Fireman has returned and handed the " Wrong Line " order back to the Driver.

If the train has stopped a short distance ahead of a signal box, and is standing in such a position that the assisting engine or breakdown van train travelling in the wrong direction will have to pass over any points worked from that box, the Driver, before issuing the "Wrong Line" order, must have it countersigned by the Signalman.

After sunset, or during fog or falling snow, or if the disabled train is left in a tunnel, the Fireman when proceeding to the signal box in advance must place 3 detonators, 10 yards apart, on the line not less than 100 yards ahead of the disabled train.

If there be no crossover road at the first signal box and it be necessary for assistance to be obtained from a signal box further ahead, the Fireman must, before proceeding to such signal box, obtain from the Signalman at the first signal box a "Wrong Line" order (Form D—*see* Rule 184) to return in the wrong direction from the signal box in advance.

A "Wrong Line" order must be issued for each occasion on which it is necessary for a train to travel in the wrong direction, as described above.

(*h*) The Driver, when returning for the portion of his train that has been left behind, or when pushing such portion of his train, or the Driver of the assisting engine or the breakdown van train as the case may be, must not pass any signal box without the permission of the Signalman.

(*i*) If, after a train has become accidentally divided between two signal boxes and the front portion has not arrived at the home signal for the box in advance, the Driver requires to set back from a point in the section, the front portion may be set back to the rear portion, provided the two portions can be recoupled, but, before moving, the Driver must send his Fireman to the Guard who is protecting the rear portion for a written authority to set back (*see* Form C at end of Rule). The Driver must retain this order.

If the engine or any vehicle of the front portion returning for the rear portion in the wrong direction will have to pass over any points worked from the signal box near which the rear portion is standing, the Guard, before issuing the " Wrong Line " order, must have it countersigned by the Signalman.

In the event of an engine assisting the train in the rear, the Guard's " Wrong Line " order must be countersigned by the Driver of that engine.

(*j*) In the case of electric trains, the Motorman, where no Assistant Motorman is employed, must carry out the duties of the Fireman.

(*k*) When it is necessary for a Motorman to issue a " Wrong Line " order, he must himself (if an Assistant Motorman is not employed) go forward and deliver it to the Signalman at the box in advance.

To be printed on PINK paper.

Form referred to in Rule 183, *clause* (f).
LONDON MIDLAND AND SCOTTISH
RAILWAY.

$\left(\begin{array}{c}\text{A supply of these Forms must}\\ \text{be kept by each Guard.}\end{array}\right)$

WRONG LINE ORDER FORM A.
GUARD TO SIGNALMAN.

To the Signalman at....................*signal box.*

Allow an engine or breakdown van train to travel in the wrong direction to my train which is stationary on the *...............line at..................
I will prevent my train being moved until the engine or breakdown van train arrives.

Catch points exist at.......................

Signed............................*Guard.*

Date..................19...   Time issued......m.

†Countersigned..............................

Driver of engine assisting in rear.

†Countersigned..............................

Signalman.

at.....................signal box.

* *Insert name of line, for example, Up or Down Main, Fast, Slow or Goods.*

† *If necessary.*

206

To be printed on GREEN paper.

Form referred to in Rule 183, *clause* (g).

LONDON MIDLAND AND SCOTTISH RAILWAY.

$\left(\begin{array}{c}\text{A supply of these Forms must}\\ \text{be kept by each Driver.}\end{array}\right)$

WRONG LINE ORDER FORM B. DRIVER TO SIGNALMAN.

To the Signalman at.....................signal box.

Allow an assisting engine or breakdown van train to proceed in the wrong direction to my train, which is stationary on the *.....................line at.................. I will not move my engine in any direction until the arrival of the assisting engine.

Catch points exist at.....................

Signed.......................*Driver.*

Date.................19... Time issued......m.

†Countersigned...............................

Signalman.

at..........................signal box.

* *Insert name of line, for example, Up or Down Main, Fast, Slow or Goods.*

† *If necessary.*

To be printed on WHITE paper.

Form referred to in Rule 183, *clause* (i).
LONDON MIDLAND AND SCOTTISH
RAILWAY.

(**A supply of these Forms must**
be kept by each Guard.)

WRONG LINE ORDER FORM C.
GUARD TO DRIVER.

To Driver of Engine No...................

I authorise you to set back to the rear portion
of your train.

Catch points exist at..................

Signed.......................*Guard.*

Date..................19... Time issued......m.

†Countersigned...............................

Driver of engine assisting in rear.

†Countersigned...............................

Signalman.

at...........................signal box.

† *If necessary.*

---

184. If, in case of accident or other exceptional
circumstance, it is necessary for a train or portion of a
train to return in the wrong direction to the signal box
in rear, or for an engine, engines coupled together,

engine and one or more brake vans, or breakdown van train coming to the assistance of a disabled train, to travel in the wrong direction to the signal box in rear, or if it is necessary for a ballast train working in section or an inspection train to return to the signal box in rear, the Guard or Fireman must first go or send some other competent person to the Signalman there, and obtain his permission in writing (see Form D at end of Rule). The Driver must not move in the wrong direction until he has received such written permission, and if the engine or train is required to travel from the signal box in advance the " Wrong Line " order must be counter-signed by the Signalman at that box.

If it is necessary before reaching the signal box for the train or portion of train returning in the wrong direction to be turned on to another line or siding, or to stop at a required point, the Signalman must show on the " Wrong Line " order the line over which the train will travel, or the point at which the train is required to stop : the Guard must be advised of the circumstances. The person returning the " Wrong Line " order form must inform the Signalman that the train, or portion of train, for which the " Wrong Line " order was issued is complete.

A " Wrong Line " order must be issued for each occasion on which it is necessary for a train to travel in the wrong direction as described above, and a separate order must be issued by the Signalman in rear of each section through which the train will pass. The " Wrong Line " order must be returned to the Signalman at the signal box at which it was issued.

Form referred to in Rules 175, clause (c), 183, clauses (f) and (g), 184 and 203.

LONDON MIDLAND AND SCOTTISH RAILWAY.

(A supply of these Forms must be kept in each signal box.)

WRONG LINE ORDER FORM D.
SIGNALMAN TO DRIVER.

To Driver of Engine No....................working ....train.

I authorise you to travel with your train on the *..................line in the wrong direction to this signal box.

Catch points exist at.........................

Signed.........................*Signalman.*

at.........................*signal box.*

Date..................19... Time issued......m.

† Countersigned...............................

Signalman.

at.....................signal box.

* Insert name of line, for example, Up or Down Main, Fast, Slow or Goods.

† If necessary.

185. (*a*) When moving in the wrong direction, as laid down in Rules 175 (*c*), 183, 184 and 216 (*j*), the Driver must proceed cautiously, travel at reduced speed, and make frequent use of the engine whistle by giving a series of " pop " whistles. A lamp must be carried on

the trailing vehicle in the direction of travel ; the lamp must show a white light after sunset or during fog or falling snow.

(*b*) When passing through a tunnel, or after sunset or during fog or falling snow, a white light must be carried on the engine or leading vehicle when moving in the wrong direction under the authority of " Wrong Line " order form A, B or C, but if the movement is performed under the authority of " Wrong Line " order form D, a red light must be carried on the leading vehicle.

(*c*) When it is necessary for two or more engines coupled together or attached to a train to travel in the wrong direction this may be done under the provisions of Rules 175 (*c*), 183 or 184, as the case may be, and when Form C or D is used the number of each engine must be shown on the form.

The " Wrong Line " order form must be shown to the Driver of each engine and delivered to and carried by the Driver of the rearmost engine in the direction of travel authorised by the form.

186.   Should catch points exist, arrangements must be made for securing them, and Drivers, when authorised to travel in the wrong direction under the circumstances referred to in Rules 175, 183 and 184, must not pass over such catch points until they have assured themselves that they are held or secured in their proper position for the train to run over them. Signalmen must, before authorising Drivers to run in the wrong direction, remind them of the existence of the catch points.

187. (*a*) In the event of any failure of, or accident to, some part of a train, it will generally be found .desirable to bring the train to a stand as quickly as possible, but whether this course can be taken with safety, and how the stoppage can best be effected, must depend on the nature of the mishap to the train, the weight and speed of the train, the gradients, curves, and other conditions applying to the line, particularly as regards the position of points and crossings. In all cases when the whole of the train remains upon the rails, it must be brought to a stand as quickly as possible.

(*b*) If the engine be defective, the sooner the train can be stopped the better. If any of the vehicles be off the rails, the brakes in the rear must be instantly applied, in order that by keeping the couplings tight the disabled vehicles may be kept up and out of the way of the vehicles behind until the force of the latter is exhausted, it being desirable that the front portion of the train should be brought slowly to a stand. The application of the front brakes might result in further damage, and great care must be exercised in their application. In all cases the application of brakes behind a disabled vehicle, or the application by the Guard of the continuous brake at the rear of a train will be attended with advantage, and rear Guards of trains fitted with the continuous brake must apply the continuous brake as well as the hand brake.

(*c*) In the event of the rear Guard not promptly applying the brakes when the Driver whistles for them, the Driver must, if his train is fitted with the continuous brake, apply the same gradually, and with judgment and care.

(*d*) Should any part of a train on which the continuous brake is not in operation become detached when in motion, the front part of the train must not be stopped if this can be avoided before the rear portion has either been stopped or is running slowly, and the rear Guard must promptly apply his brake to prevent a collision with the front portion.

(*e*) In all cases Drivers and Guards must act according to the best of their judgment and ability in the circumstances in which they are placed.

188. Should any vehicle in a train be on fire, the train must be stopped, and, if not protected by fixed signals, the Guard must protect it in compliance with Rule 178. The Fireman or the front Guard if there be two Guards, must detach the vehicles in the rear of those on fire ; the burning vehicles must be drawn forward to a distance of 50 yards at least, then uncoupled, and left properly secured, until the fire can be extinguished, to effect which every effort must be made.

12

WORKING NORMAL DOUBLE LINE TRAFFIC OVER A SINGLE LINE

Working trains in two directions over a single line can be hazardous due to the risk of a head-on collision.

On the single line Somerset & Dorset Railway, in addition to the Absolute Block system, trains had booked crossing points to pass those running in the opposite direction. Caleb Percy in his office at Glastonbury was responsible for crossing trains running out of course and was in contact with stations by means of the single-needle telegraph.

On Bank Holiday Monday 7 August 1876, the 7.10 p.m. Up Relief from Wimborne to Bath arrived at Radstock fifteen minutes earlier than Percy had calculated. Stationmaster John Jarrett tried to contact Percy by telegraph for instructions, was unable to get through and instead of waiting until an answer was received, recklessly sent it on.

Between Radstock and the next station, Wellow, a colliery siding at Foxcote had been opened the previous year. The signal box was merely for working the siding and as it had no crossing loop was only capable of passing on trains. When the 7.10 arrived at Foxcote it was held as the block ahead was still occupied by the previous Up train. In due course the block was cleared and the 7.10 sent towards Wellow.

Unfortunately at Wellow, Stationmaster James Sleep, having been on duty from 5.00 a.m., had gone off duty to quench his thirst at Midford, leaving a fifteen-year-old lad, Arthur Hillard, in charge. At 11.03 p.m. a special arrived from Bath and Hillard sent it on to Radstock, claiming that he had received 'Line Clear' from Foxcote. The two trains collided head-on, killing ten adults, two children and a guard.

The outcome of the accident was that the block system was improved at a cost of £1,100; Caleb Percy was dismissed with one month's salary in lieu of notice and James Sleep and John Jarrett were also sacked.

The fact that no electrical or mechanical safety device can altogether eliminate human mistakes is illustrated by the Abermule disaster of 26

January 1921. The 10.05 a.m. Cambrian Railways stopping train from Whitchurch to Aberystwyth was scheduled to cross the Aberystwyth to Manchester express at Abermule, though if either train was late, they crossed at an adjoining station.

The Tyer's single line electric tablet instruments were installed in the station building and not in the signal box. Although only the stationmaster and signalman were authorised to work the tablet instruments, things were slack at Abermule and in practice they were worked by anyone who was in the vicinity.

On 26 January Signalman Jones at Abermule accepted the stopping train and pressed the release, which enabled his counterpart to withdraw the necessary single line tablet. He then rang up Moat Lane Junction to enquire as to the location of the express and was told it was on its way to Newtown, the next station before Abermule.

Jones then left the instrument room and proceeded to his box at the end of the platform in order to set the road and open the level crossing gates for the stopping train.

Newtown then rang asking permission to send the express forward to Abermule. Rodgers, a junior porter, aged seventeen, pressed the release to allow Newtown to withdraw a tablet and walked to the ground frame at the opposite end of the platform from the signal box to set the road for the express to enter the passing loop. The arrival of the stopping train then diverted Rodgers from his intention to call on Signalman Jones to release the ground frame lock. Junior clerk Thompson, aged fifteen, collected the tablet from the stopping train and intended to return the tablet to the instrument, but met the stationmaster and gave it to him.

Unfortunately Stationmaster Lewis thought that the express was late and that the tablet he had been given was for the section onwards to Newtown, so handed it back to the driver of the stopping train.

The driver should have examined the tablet to make sure that it was the correct one for the section ahead, but failed to do so. Signalman Jones, knowing that the express was running to time, was surprised when he saw the stationmaster hand over the tablet to the stopping train driver, but had utter faith in the infallibility of Tyer's system.

The road was set for the stopping train to proceed and it went on its way. The two trains collided, killing fifteen passengers, the crew of the stopping train engine and the express guard. The express driver checked his tablet and found it correct but discovered that the one carried on the stopping train engine was for the previous section.

Colonel Pringle, the Board of Trade inspecting officer, made recommendations: that the single line electric tablet instruments should only be in the signal box and that each instrument be interlocked with the starting signal to prevent it from being pulled off until the instrument had been cleared

Just as there were stringent precautions to prevent trains from colliding on single lines, so the Rule Book provided for working normal double-line traffic over a single line. Such an event could occur when work was taking place such as track renewal, or a slipping embankment or cutting being stabilised.

WORKING TRAFFIC OF A DOUBLE LINE OVER A SINGLE LINE OF RAILS DURING REPAIRS OR OBSTRUCTION.

189. When the traffic of a double line has to be worked over a single line of rails during repairs or owing to an obstruction, the following precautions must be adopted.

190. Single line working should be confined to the shortest length practicable and, whenever possible, between crossover roads where there are fixed signals, but in the event of a crossover road not protected by fixed signals being used the provisions of Rule 199 must be observed.

191. A competent person must be appointed as Pilotman, who must wear, round his left arm above the elbow, a red armlet with the word " Pilotman " shown thereon in white letters, thus :—

If this armlet is not immediately available the

Pilotman must wear a red flag in the position indicated until the proper armlet is obtained.

192. Except as provided in Rule 200. clause (*f*). and in the first paragraph of Rule 206, no train must be allowed to enter upon or foul any portion of the single line without the Pilotman being present and riding upon the engine, except when a train is to be followed by one or more trains in the same direction, in which case the Pilotman must personally order each train to proceed and must ride upon the engine of the last train. When an engine supplied specially for the use of the Pilotman is coupled to a train it must be attached to the front unless it is necessary for such engine to be used for banking purposes where the use of bank engines is authorised. If the Pilotman travels on a train with two or more engines he must ride upon the rearmost engine. If the Pilotman travels on an electric train, rail motor or motor train he must ride with the Driver.

The Pilotman must show himself on each occasion to the Signalman at each box he passes, to the Hand-signalman at catch and other points and to Fogsignalmen when on duty

193. (*a*) The Station Masters or other responsible persons at both ends of the obstructed section must communicate with each other by the most expeditious means, agree as to who shall arrange for pilot-working, and have a clear understanding as to the arrangements to be put into operation.

(*b*) It will generally be found more expeditious for

the Station Master or other responsible person in advance of the obstruction to undertake the arrangements, as the Pilotman with the single line forms can then make his first journey by train or trolley, if either is available, on the proper running line. Under no circumstances must a train or trolley be allowed to run over the unobstructed line *in the wrong direction* until the Pilotman's form is signed by the Signalman at each end of the single line section, and also at any intermediate signal box.

(c) The person arranging single line working must fill up, sign, and address single line forms (*see* page 258 for specimen form) to—

> (i.) The Signalmen controlling the crossover roads between which single line working is to be put in operation.
>
> (ii.) The Signalman at any signal box and the Station Master at any station that is intermediate on the line which is to be worked as a single line, provided such signal box or station is open or likely to be open during the time single line working is in operation.
>
> (iii.) The person who will act as Pilotman.
>
> (iv.) The Station Master at each end of the single line, except where the signal box at which single line working commences or finishes is not at a station and the ordinary working at the station will not be interfered with.

These forms must be handed to the Pilotman who must also sign all the forms issued and deliver the necessary form to the Signalman in charge of the crossover road at which the single line working commences and then proceed to the other end of the section. The Pilotman on his way must verbally inform persons in charge of level crossings, Gangers, Lengthmen and any other men at work on the line, that single line working is about to be commenced and which line will be used; he must also leave the necessary form with the person in charge of any intermediate signal box or station then open. On his arrival at the other end of the single line section the Pilotman must deliver the necessary forms to the Station Master and Signalman. Each person when receiving the form must sign the Pilotman's form. Trains may then be allowed to pass over the single line by the permission and under the control of the Pilotman.

Where the crossover road at each end of the line to be worked as a single line is under the control of one Signalman, these instructions must be observed, except that the single line form will be issued to the Signalman concerned.

Whenever it is temporarily necessary to work the traffic over two up or two down lines in those cases where the up or down lines adjoin one another, the special form shown on pages 260 and 261 must be used.

When a Station Master himself acts as Pilotman he must retain only the Pilotman's form, and unless his station comes within the exception mentioned in section (iv.) of this clause (c), he must address and give a form to the person he leaves in charge of his station.

Should any intermediate signal boxes or stations be opened after single line working has commenced, the Pilotman must, as soon as practicable, advise the persons in charge of such places that single line working is in operation. He must also hand forms signed by the person who arranged the single line working and himself, to the Signalmen and Station Masters concerned, who must sign the form held by the Pilotman.

(d) Station Masters and persons in charge issuing and receiving single line forms will be responsible for the Inspectors, Signalmen, and others concerned at their station being made acquainted with the circumstances immediately, and instructed in their necessary duties.

Twelve single line forms must be kept in a convenient place at each station, and at every signal box where there is a crossover road, so as to be available at any time.

(e) **When single line working is put into operation an entry must be made in the train register books in the signal boxes stating the time the single line working was put into operation, between what points, and the time ordinary working is resumed. These entries must be signed by the Pilotman.**

194. (a) At each end of the obstructed line 3 detonators must be placed on such line 10 yards apart, $\frac{1}{4}$ mile, or more if necessary, from the point where single line working commences (*see* diagram on page 237). When, however, the distance from the obstruction to the point where single line working

commences is less than $\frac{1}{4}$-mile, the detonators in rear of the obstruction must be placed as far from the obstruction as circumstances permit, and the detonators in advance of the obstruction must be placed as far from the crossover road as circumstances permit.

(*b*) A red flag by day, and a red light after sunset or during fog or falling snow must also be placed on the obstructed line near to the detonators. When lights are used these must show a Danger signal towards both the obstruction and the crossover road.

(c) During fog or falling snow a Fogsignalman must, whenever possible, be provided at the distant signal for the obstructed line operated from the box at which the trains are crossed to their proper line and he must place a detonator for each train travelling in the wrong direction on the line which is being used as a single line, opposite the distant signal and exhibit a hand Caution signal, in order that Drivers approaching the facing crossover road may be advised of their position. The Pilotman must instruct the Fogsignalman accordingly. Until a Fogsignalman is stationed at this signal the Pilotman must specially warn all Drivers that the Fogsignalman has not taken up duty.

If a fog or snowstorm occurs when single line working is in operation, the Signalman must, when this Fogsignalman commences duty, inform him of the single line working, and instruct him to act in accordance with the preceding paragraph.

The signalman at any intermediate signal box must instruct the Fogsignalmen, where employed, to place

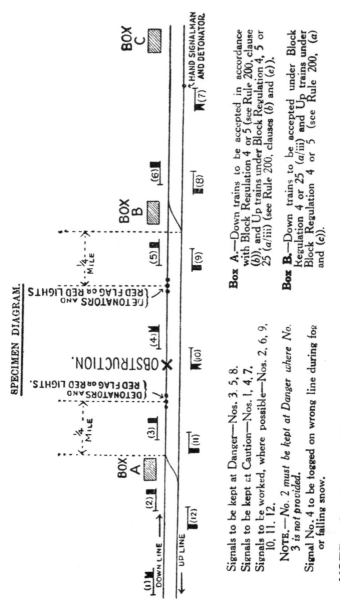

SPECIMEN DIAGRAM.

Signals to be kept at Danger—Nos. 3, 5, 8.

Signals to be kept at Caution—Nos. 1, 4, 7.

Signals to be worked, where possible—Nos. 2, 6, 9, 10, 11, 12.

NOTE.—*No. 2 must be kept at Danger where No. 3 is not provided.*

Signal No. 4 to be fogged on wrong line during fog or falling snow.

Box A.—Down trains to be accepted in accordance with Block Regulation 4 or 5 (see Rule 200, clause (b)), and Up trains under Block Regulation 4, 5 or 25 (a/iii) (see Rule 200, clauses (b) and (e)).

Box B.—Down trains to be accepted under Block Regulation 4 or 25 (a/iii) and Up trains under Block Regulation 4 or 5 (see Rule 200, (a) and (e)).

NOTE.—On the Great Western Railway 2 detonators are used at the distant signal (No. 7).

223

the detonators on the line being used as a single line for trains running in the direction to which the signal applies.

Note.—*On the Great Western Railway 2 detonators, 10 yards apart, are used at the distant signal referred to in clause (c).*

195. (*a*) All points, including spring points and unworked trailing points, which become facing points to trains running over the single line, must be secured so as to ensure trains passing safely over them. In the case of spring points and unworked trailing points, the person instituting the single line working must arrange for a competent man to be appointed to hand-signal the trains over them.

(*b*) The person instituting the single line working must arrange for all catch points in the single line, except those worked from a signal box and required to be operated for the protection of another line, to be closed and firmly secured before single line working is commenced ; he must also arrange for a man, provided with hand signals and detonators, to be placed at such points with instructions to see that they are continuously kept closed and secured during the whole of the time that single line working is in operation.

In the case of catch points worked from a signal box and required to be operated for the protection of another line, the person instituting the single line working must arrange for a man, provided with hand signals and detonators, to be placed at such points with instructions to see that they are properly closed and firmly secured for the passage of each train approaching them in the facing direction.

196. (a) When a train is approaching catch points, spring points or unworked trailing points in the facing direction, the man at the points must, provided they are right for the train to pass over them, give the Driver a green hand signal held steadily.

(b) The Pilotman must satisfy himself that the Driver is aware of the location of these points, and Drivers must not pass over any of them in the facing direction until they have received a signal to do so from the man at the points.

197. (a) The following signals must be kept at Danger and Drivers must not pass them except as shown :—

Signals to be kept at Danger.	May be passed.
(i.) The signal immediately controlling the entrance to the single line for trains travelling in the right direction.	When instructed by Pilotman.
(ii.) The signal immediately protecting the crossover road where trains cross from the single line to their proper line of rails.	When instructed by Signalman ; or by Pilotman or Hand-signalman under the authority of the Signalman.

(iii.) The signal controlling the entrance to the obstructed line where such signal is situated ahead of the crossover road at which trains are crossed from the right line to proceed along the single line.	When instructed by Signalman (or by Pilotman or Hand-signalman under the authority of the Signalman) to draw ahead on to obstructed line. When instructed by Pilotman to proceed along single line in wrong direction.
(iv.) The signal controlling the entrance to the obstructed line where such signal is situated in rear of the crossover road at which trains are crossed from the right line to proceed along the single line and there is not another stop signal in advance	When instructed by Signalman ; or by Pilotman or Hand-signalman under the authority of the Signalman.

(*b*) The other signals applying to the obstructed line, situated between the two crossover roads, except as otherwise provided in clauses (*d*), (*e*) and (*f*) of this Rule, must, where practicable, be maintained at Danger and may be passed by Drivers without special authority.

The other signals applying to the single line must, where practicable, be worked.

(*c*) Where it is necessary for trains to approach a

junction on the single line in the wrong direction a Handsignalman must be stationed opposite the junction home signal and he must keep one detonator on the rail of the single line, and exhibit a hand Danger signal to stop any train approaching on the single line in the wrong direction until the Signalman authorises him to permit the train to pass the signal at Danger. Where the junction home signal is so situated that a train coming to a stand at it would foul the junction, the Handsignalman must be stationed well clear of the junction.

NOTE.—*On the Great Western Railway 2 detonators, 10 yards apart, are used at the junction home signal referred to in clause (c).*

(*d*) Where more than one home signal is provided to facilitate the acceptance of trains, and such trains approach these signals on the single line in the wrong direction, a Handsignalman must be stationed opposite the outermost home signal. This signal must, whenever possible, be worked, and the Handsignalman must keep one detonator on the rail of the single line and exhibit a hand Danger signal to stop any train approaching this signal until it is lowered or the Signalman authorises him to permit the train to pass the signal at Danger.

NOTE.—*On the Great Western Railway 2 detonators, 10 yards apart, are used at the outermost home signal referred to in clause (d).*

(*e*) At intermediate boxes, when block working is maintained, the fixed signals must (except where the lock and block or other similar system of signalling is in operation) be worked for trains passing over the single line in both directions. Should a train have been brought to a stand on the obstructed line at an intermediate box and have to remain there during single line working the Signalman must instruct the Driver not to move until verbally instructed to do so although the signal at which his train is standing may be lowered. Where the lock and block or other similar system is in force or when block working is suspended, the fixed signals must be kept at Danger and the Signalman must handsignal Drivers past the signals when the line is clear for trains to proceed.

(f) The fixed signals protecting level crossings must, where possible, be worked for trains passing over the single line in both directions. Where the signals in either or both directions cannot be worked, a hand signal must be given by the Crossing Keeper or other appointed person to the Driver to pass the stop signal when the line is clear for the train to proceed.

198. (a) Block working must be maintained whenever possible in connection with single line working, but when it is necessary to suspend block working this must be done only by the person who arranges the single line working.

Block working must, however, be maintained or the provisions of Block Regulation 25, clause (a/iii.), observed, or the Pilotman must accompany every train passing over the single line when any of the following conditions apply—

Fog or falling snow.
The gradients are heavy
A tunnel or movable bridge intervenes.

Where block working is maintained, up trains must be signalled on the up line block instruments and down trains on the down line block instruments.

(*b*) When block working is maintained, and the block indicator for the obstructed line is at the " Train on line " position, the Signalman at the box in advance of the obstruction must, in order that the block signalling of trains in both directions on the single line may be carried on as laid down in the foregoing paragraph, release the block indicator in accordance with the following instructions :—

(i.) If the Station Master in advance of the obstruction arranges the single line working and the Pilotman is conveyed by train to the signal box in rear, the Signalman there must, after receiving the single line form and provided the train has arrived complete, give the " Train out of section " signal, and the Signalman in advance of the obstruction, after acknowledging such signal, must release the block indicator for the obstructed line.

If the Pilotman is not conveyed through the section by train, he must, when the arrangements for commencing single line working have been completed, instruct the Signalman at the box in rear of the obstruction to so inform the Signalman at the box in advance ; the latter Signalman must then release the block indicator for the obstructed line.

(ii.) When the Station Master in rear of the obstruction arranges the single line working, the

Pilotman, when handing the single line form to the Signalman in advance of the obstruction, must instruct him to release the block indicator for the obstructed line.

NOTE.—*Clause (b) is not applicable to lines worked on the lock and block or other similar system.*

(c) When block working is maintained during single line working and track circuiting is provided in either the obstructed line or the line used as a single line, the Lineman must, except where instructions are issued to the contrary, be requested in writing by the person arranging single line working to disconnect the control of the track circuit over the block indicators and signals if either of the following conditions obtain:—

> (i.) The signals which require to be worked are locked by the occupation of a track circuit in the obstructed line.
>
> (ii.) The block indicator is likely to be wrongly placed to the "Train on line" or normal position by a train travelling in the wrong direction over a track circuit provided in the line used as a single line, or wrongly maintained at "Train on line" or normal position by the occupation of the obstructed line.

If it is necessary to commence single line working before the arrival of the Lineman and the block indicators are thus affected, they must be regarded as out of use and the provisions of Block Regulation 25 observed.

Before double line working is resumed the control of the track circuit over the block indicators and signals must be restored, or the provisions of Rule 77, clause (e), observed.

199. In the event of a crossover road not protected by fixed signals being used for single line working, a competent man, with hand signals and detonators, must be placed at least ¾ mile on each side of the crossover road to signal in place of distant signals, and a man, similarly equipped, at each side of the crossover road to signal in place of home signals. Each man must place and maintain one detonator on the line concerned, and the man acting in place of the distant signal must exhibit a hand Caution signal, and the man acting in place of the home signal must exhibit a hand Danger signal to stop all trains approaching the single line. Should the distance of ¾ mile fall within a tunnel, or close to the mouth of a tunnel nearer to the obstruction, or in any other position where, owing to the formation of the line, or to some other circumstance, the Driver of an approaching train would be unable to obtain a good and distant view of the hand signal, then the detonator must be placed and the hand signal exhibited at the end of the tunnel farther from the crossover road, or at such a distance over and above the prescribed distance of ¾ mile as may be necessary to ensure the Driver obtaining a good and distant view of such signal.

NOTE.—*On the Great Western Railway 2 detonators, 10 yards apart, are used.*

200. (a) Before single line working is put in operation, the Signalman at each end of the single line must, when practicable, advise the Signalman at the box in rear. Where the line is blocked between boxes " A " and " B," as shown in diagram on page 237, trains travelling over the single line in the wrong direction must be accepted at box " B " in accordance with Block Regulation 4 or 25, clause (a/iii.). The Signalman at box " B " may, except during fog or falling snow, allow a train to approach the single line from box " C " in accordance with Block Regulation 4, provided the Pilotman is present at box " B " and block working is being maintained in each direction. The Pilotman must, on each occasion that he arrives at box " B," sign the train register book, and must not leave that end of the single line until any train accepted under Block Regulation 4 from box " C " has arrived. The Signalman must have a complete understanding with the Pilotman before accepting a train in accordance with this Regulation.

When the line is not clear in accordance with Block Regulation 4, or the Pilotman is not present, or during fog or falling snow such trains must, except as shown in clause (c), be accepted by the Signalman at box " B " in accordance with Block Regulation 5. The Signalman at box " C " must stop each train proceeding towards the single line that is accepted by the Signalman at box " B " in accordance with Block Regulation 5, and advise the Driver that single line working is in operation at the box in advance.

Except as shown in clause (c), a Handsignalman must be placed outside the distant signal for box " B " for trains approaching from box " C " (*see* diagram on page 237), and he must place one detonator on the rail for each approaching train, and exhibit a hand Caution signal. When, however, the distant signal is on the same post as a stop signal a red hand signal must be exhibited by the Hand-signalman to Drivers of approaching trains if the stop signal is at Danger, and a yellow hand signal if the stop signal is at Clear.

NOTE.—*On the Great Western Railway 2 detonators, 10 yards apart, are used at the distant signal referred to above.*

(*b*) The Signalman at the box controlling the crossover road where trains are crossed from the obstructed line to proceed along the single line in the wrong direction may, except during fog or falling snow, allow a train to approach the obstructed line in accordance with Block Regulation 4, but, during fog or falling snow, or when the line is not clear in accordance with Block Regulation 4 but is clear to the home signal, a train may be allowed to approach in accordance with Block Regulation 5. Trains approaching this box on the single line must be accepted under Block Regulation 4 or 25, clause (*a*/iii.), except as otherwise provided for in clause (*e*) of this Rule.

(*c*) Where an additional home signal is provided for acceptance purposes, for trains approaching either the obstructed line or the line being used as a single line, such trains must be signalled as under normal working, and, in the case of trains approaching the single line it will not be necessary to place a Handsignalman outside the distant signal applicable to the line upon which the single line working is in operation. During fog or falling snow, however, all trains approaching the single line must be accepted under Block Regulation 5 until the Fogsignalmen, appointed for the distant signal and the outermost home signal for the box at which the single line working commences, have arrived at their posts ; the Signalman at the box in rear must stop each train accepted under Block Regulation 5 and advise the Driver that single line working is in operation at the box in advance.

(d) Where one of the lines is blocked between the crossover roads at boxes " B " and " C " or " B " and " D " (*see* diagram on following page) and trains approach " B " from " C " or " D " in the wrong direction, all trains from " A," " C " and " D " must be accepted at box " B " in accordance with Block Regulation 4 or 25, clause (a/iii.).

Where one of the lines is blocked between the cross-over roads at boxes " B " and " C " or " B " and " D " (*see* diagram on following page) and trains approach " B " in the right direction, all trains from " C " and " D " must, except as provided in the third paragraph of this clause (d) and in clause (e), be accepted at box " B " in accordance with Block Regulation 4 or 25, clause (a/iii.), and trains from " A " must be accepted in accordance with the first sentence of clause (b) of this Rule.

Where trains on the single line approach " B " in the right direction and in normal working Block Regulation 5 is authorised on the unobstructed route from " C " or " D " (*see* diagram on following page), trains approaching " B " on the unobstructed route may be accepted in accordance with Block Regulation 5, or 25, clause (a/iii.), provided block working or the provisions of Block Regulation 25, clause (a/iii.), are observed in connection with trains approaching " B " on the single line.

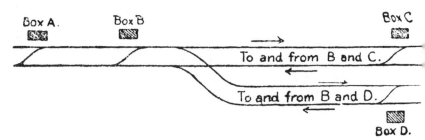

(e) Where in normal working Block Regulation 5 is authorised on a line used as a single line, trains travelling over the single line in the right direction may be accepted in accordance with Block Regulation 5 or 25, clause (a/iii.)

(f) The crossover road through which trains are crossed from the obstructed line to proceed along the single line in the wrong direction may be used without the Pilotman being present.

201. When block working or Block Regulation 25, clause (a/iii.), is in operation the Pilotman must obtain the permission of the Signalman before allowing a train to enter upon the single line.

202. (a) No train must be allowed to enter upon the single line without the Driver and Guard having first

been informed by the Pilotman that single line working is in operation and between what points. When, however, a train requires only to pass over or foul a portion of the single line at a junction it will not be necessary to convey this intimation to the Driver and Guard, and the signals may be lowered and the train allowed to pass without being stopped.

(b) When a train is followed by one or more trains in the same direction and block working is suspended, the Driver and Guard of each train must be so advised by the Pilotman and instructed to proceed cautiously.

203. When it is necessary for any movement to be made from the portion of the obstructed line situated between the 3 detonators placed $\frac{1}{4}$ mile from each crossover road, such movement must not be made past the detonators towards either crossover road until a clear understanding has been come to with the Signalman controlling the crossover road in advance, or a "Wrong Line" order (Form D, see Rule 184) has been obtained for a movement towards the crossover road in rear.

204. Trains must be run over the single line cautiously and at reduced speed and Drivers must make frequent use of the whistle by giving a series of " pop " whistles. When passing through a tunnel, or after sunset or during fog or falling snow, trains must carry a red head light. These instructions, however, will not apply to trains which only require to pass to or from the unobstructed route at a junction.

The speed of trains travelling over the single line in the wrong direction must not exceed 10 miles per hour when passing over any points which become facing points, and Drivers must be prepared to act on any hand signal which may be given them.

205. (a) Should it be necessary to change the Pilotman, the person who arranged the single line working must issue fresh forms on which must be inserted the name of the new Pilotman to whom the necessary forms must be handed in the presence of the Pilotman who is being relieved, and the latter must at the same time hand his form to the new Pilotman. The Pilotman who has been relieved will then cease to act as Pilotman and must not ride upon any engine, or with the Driver of any electric train, rail motor or motor train, travelling over the single line. The new Pilotman must sign and deliver the fresh forms, obtain the necessary signatures, and at the same time withdraw the old forms which must afterwards be delivered by him to the person who arranged the single line working.

(b) Should the Signalmen be changed during single line working the man coming on duty must be made acquainted, by the man going off duty, with the arrangements in force. If the Pilotman is at the end of the section at which the change of Signalmen is being made the Signalman coming on duty must sign the form held by the Pilotman before taking charge of the signal box. If, however, the Pilotman is not at that end of the section, the Signalman coming on duty may take charge, but before doing so must sign the single line form then in the signal box in the presence of the Signalman going off duty who will be responsible for seeing this is done, and the Signalman coming on duty must sign the Pilotman's form at the first opportunity.

When commencing single line working the Pilotman must ascertain the time at which the Signalmen change duty and as soon as practicable arrange for those coming on duty later to sign the single line form held by him.

206. Where the single line working terminates at a junction, trains passing the junction signal box to and from the unobstructed route having to pass over or foul a portion of the line being used as a single line, may be allowed to do so without the Pilotman being present, provided block working or the provisions of Block Regulation 25, clause (a/iii.), are maintained in all directions. In such circumstances the Handsignal-man referred to in Rule 200, clause (a), must not be employed at the distant signal worked from the junction box, but during fog or falling snow the usual fog-signalling arrangements must be carried out in connection with such signal.

NOTE.—*The above paragraph does not apply on the Great Western and Southern Companies' lines where the working will be carried out in accordance with the following arrangements which are only applicable on those lines.*

(i.) Where the single line working terminates at a junction (*see* diagram on page 253), and one line is obstructed between the crossover roads at boxes " B " and " C " or " B " and " D," necessitating trains passing box " B " to or from the unobstructed route having to pass over or foul a portion of the line being used as a single line, or to foul the crossover road, an additional Pilotman to be known as the Junction Pilotman, may be appointed to facilitate working at the junction, in which case the Pilotman referred to in Rule 191 will be called the Section Pilotman.

The Station Masters or other responsible persons at both ends of the obstructed section must communicate with each other and agree as to whether or not a Junction Pilotman is required.

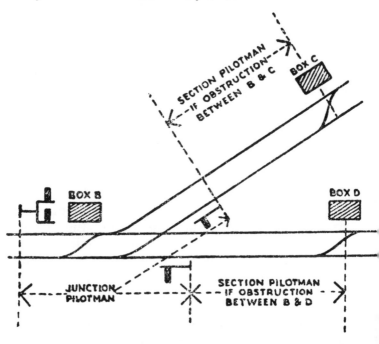

A Junction Pilotman may also be appointed at an intermediate junction not provided with a crossover road where trains cross or foul the single line.

The Junction Pilotman must wear two armlets round his left arm, one above and one below the elbow. If these armlets are not immediately available he must wear two red flags until the proper armlets are obtained.

The Section Pilotman will be responsible for passing trains over the single line except between the stop signal, or Handsignalman immediately protecting the junction, and the crossover road at the junction.

When a Junction Pilotman is appointed all the forms used must be the pink forms (*see* page 259 for specimen form), and they must be issued and signed in accordance with Rule 193. The Junction Pilotman must also be given a single line form, and he must sign the forms held by the Section Pilotman, the Junction Signalman and the Station Master at the junction, and they must sign the form held by him. If single line working has been established by the issue of white forms and it becomes necessary to appoint a Junction Pilotman, these forms must be withdrawn and pink forms issued. The Section Pilotman must deliver the fresh forms and obtain the necessary signatures, and at the same time withdraw the old forms. The issue of the new forms must only be done by the person who arranged the single line working, to whom the Section Pilotman must deliver the old forms.

Twelve of the pink forms must be kept in a convenient place at each station and signal box where it may be necessary to arrange for a Junction Pilotman so as to be available at any time.

(ii.) The Section Pilotman must instruct the Driver

of every train passing over his section of the single line towards the junction not to pass any stop signal worked from the junction signal box until the signal is lowered or he receives authority by hand signal to do so, and in the case of the stop signal immediately protecting the junction (or the Handsignalman at the junction where one is provided) until personally authorised to do so by the Junction Pilotman. Where in normal working trains are allowed to approach the junction in accordance with Block Regulation 4 from the direction in which single line working is in operation whilst other trains are permitted to cross or foul the junction through which the approaching train has to run, this working may remain in operation during single line working, and trains may also be allowed to leave the signal box in rear under such circumstances when Block Regulation 25, clause (a/iii.), is in operation on the single line over which the Section Pilotman is responsible for working.

(iii.) The Junction Pilotman will be responsible for piloting all trains coming from, or going to, the single line controlled by the Section Pilotman, or personally authorising the Drivers of such trains to proceed, and for authorising all shunting operations within the signals immediately protecting the junction, and in these circumstances the provisions of Rule 200, clause (f), will not apply.

The Section Pilotman and the Junction Pilotman must confer with each other as necessary.

Unless a Junction Pilotman is appointed, the Pilotman referred to in Rule 191 must, except as provided in Rule 200, clause (f), also control the movement of all trains running upon or fouling the portion of single line at the junction.

(iv.) A Junction Pilotman must not be appointed unless block working or the provisions of Block Regulation 25, clause (a/iii.), will be maintained in all directions.

(v.) The Junction Signalman before accepting a train or permitting a movement to take place over or to foul any portion of the single line controlled by the Junction Pilotman, must have a complete understanding with the Junction Pilotman and satisfy himself that any train brought to a stand at any of the signals protecting the junction is well clear of any other line or crossing.

(vi.) A Handsignalman must not be employed at the distant signal worked from the junction signal box applicable to the line upon which single line working is in operation, but during fog or falling snow the usual fogsignalling arrangements must be carried out in connection with such signal.

207. (a) When both lines are obstructed and it becomes necessary to work trains up to the obstruction on both sides for the transfer of passengers or any other purpose, single line working must be arranged on both sides between the nearest crossover road and the obstruction, and a Pilotman appointed to act on each side ; a responsible person must, where possible, also be placed in charge at the obstruction.

(b) Two competent men, provided with the necessary hand signals and detonators, must be appointed to protect the obstruction, one on each side.

(*c*) When one line is cleared, arrangements must be made for single line working between the crossover roads on each side of the obstruction. Both Pilotmen must proceed with the first train over the line which has been cleared, and the person who is appointed Pilotman for that line must withdraw all the single line forms previously in use, at the same time as he delivers the new forms.

208. (*a*) When the line is clear and double line working can be resumed all the forms issued for the single line working must be collected by the Pilotman. These forms must afterwards be sent to the **Divisional Superintendent of Operation, or in the case of the Northern Division the Operating Manager.**

For the purpose of collecting the forms the Pilotman may use, in the proper direction, the line which had been obstructed. He must, however, before taking a train over that line have a clear understanding with all concerned.

(*b*) When block working has been maintained, normal double line working may be resumed as soon as the single line forms have been collected. If, however, block working has been suspended and is about to be resumed, the first train travelling over the line which has been obstructed, and the first train travelling over the line which has been used as a single line must be dealt with by the Signalman in the same manner as the last train allowed to proceed through a section in which there has been a failure of the block instruments.—*See* Block Regulation 25, clause (*b*).

(Special form referred to in Rule 193, clause (c)).

LONDON MIDLAND AND SCOTTISH RAILWAY.

SINGLE LINE WORKING DURING REPAIRS OR OBSTRUCTION.

This special form must be filled up and used whenever it is temporarily necessary to work the traffic over two up or two down lines, in those cases where the two or more up or down lines adjoin one another.

....Station.

.....................................19 .

(1) The.....................................lines being blocked between
.......................and.......................all.......................traffic will pass
between these two places on the.......................line under the ordinary
block regulations.

(2) The.......................traffic will pass between these two places on
the.......................line, which will be worked as a single line under the
usual single line regulations, with Pilotman.

(3) ....will act as Pilotman between.......................
and.......................and no train must be allowed to pass on the.............
.................line unless he is present and personally orders the train to start.

(4) ....will take charge of all trains passing over the
.......................line between.......................and.......................
and no train must be allowed to pass on to this portion of the line unless it is
accompanied by.............................

NOTE.—*The arrangement detailed in the last clause will only be necessary where the traffic has to be worked over a short length of single line at one end of the blocked section and under the control of one signal box. (See diagram below.)   If such an arrangement is not necessary the paragraph must be deleted.*

*(5) { (a) Block working or Block Regulation 25, clause (a/iii.), is in operation.
{ (b) Block working is suspended.
Strike out sentence (a) or (b) not applicable.

(6) This order is to remain in force until withdrawn by the Pilotman.

†(7) Catch points, spring points, or unworked trailing points exist at.............
.................and arrangements have been made for working as directed in Rules
195 and 196.

† *Strike out sentence if no such points exist.*

(Signed).......................................

Diagram referred to in Note under clause 4.

In the above diagram the up slow and up fast lines being blocked all down traffic will pass over the down slow line, and all up traffic will pass over the down fast line under the control of the Pilotman at A. A man will be appointed at B to control all movements over the length of single line between C and D.

Noted by...
Noted by...
Noted by...
Noted by...
Noted by...
Noted by...
Noted by...
Noted by...
Noted by...
Noted by...Pilotman.

(8) Where there are parallel lines, twelve of these special forms must be kept at each station, in a convenient place, and at every signal box where there is a cross-over road, so as to be available at any moment, whether night or day.

(9) The single line form held by the Pilotman must be countersigned by the Signalman in charge at either end of the single line, by the Signalman in charge of any intermediate signal box, and by the Station Masters or others in charge of any stations directly concerned in the single line working.

(10) The Pilotman must see that each of the men signing the form retains a copy for himself.

(11) In the event of a Station Master himself acting as Pilotman, he must address and give a copy of the form to the person he leaves in charge of his station.

(12) Station Masters and persons in charge receiving this form will be held responsible that the Inspectors, Signalmen, and others concerned at their station are immediately acquainted with the circumstances, and are instructed in their necessary duties.

The additional precautions referred to in Rules 189 to 208 must be carried out where applicable to this special working.

13

THE SAFE CONVEYANCE OF EXPLOSIVES

Railways have always taken great care when conveying explosives and no serious accident has occurred attributed to their passage, but there have been several instances when trains were stationary. A heavy loss of life could have occurred on 2 January 1946. Ammunition was being transferred from lorries to railway wagons in an Army depot at Savernake Forest, when a violent explosion destroyed some wagons and set others ablaze. Eight soldiers were killed and fires threatened not just the train being loaded, but a fully loaded train alongside. Ninety-six wagons containing a total of 2,000 tons of explosives were threatened and had these been detonated, many lives would have been lost in nearby Marlborough.

Captain Kenneth Biggs personally uncoupled a blazing ammunition wagon and with another officer, pushed it to safety and extinguished the blaze. Biggs and Acting Staff Sergeant Rogerson worked through the night to ensure that all the fires in every burning wagon were extinguished and those blazing too fiercely were shunted out of harm's way. Biggs and Rogerson were both awarded the George Cross.

CONVEYANCE BY GOODS TRAINS OF EXPLOSIVES AND DANGEROUS GOODS.

240. The following instructions must be observed by Guards and others with respect to the conveyance of vehicles containing explosives and other dangerous goods :—

(1.) Each person engaged in loading, unloading, or conveying explosives or other dangerous goods must observe all necessary precautions for the prevention of accident by fire or explosion, and when loading or unloading explosives into or out of a gunpowder van must wear, whilst in the van, the magazine boots provided. He must not allow any unauthorised person to have access to such goods ; must abstain from smoking or any act whatever which tends to cause fire or explosion, and is not reasonably necessary for the loading, unloading, or conveyance ; and must prevent any other person from committing any such act. Further, he must not have upon him any matches or means of striking a light.

(2.) In loading or unloading any explosive, the casks and packages containing the same must, as far as practicable, be passed from hand to hand, and not rolled upon the ground, and in no case must any such casks or packages be rolled unless clean hides, cloths or sheets have been previously laid down on the platform or ground over which the same are to be rolled. Casks or packages containing explosives must not be thrown or dropped, but must be carefully deposited and stowed in such a manner as to prevent any displacement of the casks or packages during transit.

(3.) Casks, drums or other receptacles which are unsound or leaking must not be accepted for conveyance. If leakage from receptacles containing dangerous goods occurs in transit, such receptacles must, if other goods are in the same vehicle, be unloaded and the circumstances reported by the most expeditious means to the District Manager for Chemist's advice.

(4.) Inflammable liquids, oily rags, oily waste, oily paper, oily canvas, oily mill sweepings, and similar goods must wherever possible be loaded in separate vehicles (iron-bottomed vehicles being used in all cases when available), which must be kept as far away as practicable from vehicles containing other goods.

Before loading inflammable liquids or empties which have contained inflammable liquids the vehicles must be swept free from all litter which might be readily ignited.

(5.) When dealing with liquefied chlorine in drums (gross weight approximately between 10 cwts. and 2 tons each) the following conditions must be strictly adhered to in addition to those contained in the Dangerous Goods Classification :—

(a) The drums must be conveyed in through vehicles to destination and not transhipped.

(b) They must as far as practicable be dealt with entirely in the open.

(c) They must be adequately secured and scotched to prevent rolling in the vehicles.

(d) Suitable hooked chains for use in unloading must be sent to destination station by the sending station in the same vehicle as the drums. In the case of any emergency in which it is necessary to remove these drums from the wagon, only such cranes and hook-chains as have been certified to have a lifting power of not less than two tons must be used.

(e) The types of vehicles used must be such that the unloading can be performed without the drum at any time being lifted to a height exceeding 6 feet from the rail level.

(f) Vehicles containing drums of liquefied chlorine must not contain any corrosive or heavy articles likely to damage the drums or other articles likely to be damaged by chlorine, and must have affixed a label or labels bearing the following :—

LIQUID CHLORINE.

Handle with great care.

In the event of leakage of Gas keep on the windward side, remove wagon to as open a space as possible, and immediately telegraph or telephone to Traffic Department.

In the case of any emergency in which it is necessary to remove these drums from the wagon, only such cranes and hook-chains as have been certified to have a lifting power of not less than 2 tons must be used.

(g) If the drums are carted by the Railway Company the unloading at the consignee's premises must be performed entirely by and at the responsibility of the consignee.

(6.) Gunpowder vans must in every case be locked when sent loaded with explosives, and, except when a standard lock is used, the key must be forwarded to the receiving station.

The vans must be kept clean and nothing must be conveyed in them except explosives and the magazine boots.

(7.) Explosives for branch stations, or for any station not on the direct route to be taken by the vehicle, must not be sent in small lots requiring transhipment, unless they are packed in metallic cases or cylinders, and when explosives require to be transhipped the transhipment must be effected as speedily as possible.

(8.) Distinctive labels for explosives, inflammable liquids and dangerous goods, respectively, are provided, and on no account must vehicles containing such traffics, except explosives in metallic cases or cylinders, be allowed to travel unless one of the appropriate labels is securely affixed on each side, in order that the Guard may be aware of the contents.

(9.) Whenever vehicles containing explosives, inflammable liquids, or other dangerous goods have to be forwarded by train, the special attention of the Guard must be called to the vehicles by a duly authorised person, and the Guard will be responsible for the proper observance of these instructions while the goods are being conveyed on the train, and until they are delivered into the safe custody of the station staff.

(10.) Not more than five vehicles containing explosives must be conveyed by any one train at any one time. Vehicles containing explosives or highly inflammable liquids or tank wagons containing compressed liquefied gases must be marshalled as near the middle of the train as possible. Vehicles containing explosives and tank wagons containing compressed liquefied gases must not be placed on the train near to vehicles containing inflammable liquids or other traffic of an inflammable nature.

(11.) Open vehicles conveying explosives contained in metallic cases or cylinders must be sheeted to protect the contents against risk of fire.

Vehicles containing inflammable liquids, or empty vessels which have been used for inflammable liquids, must not be sheeted, except in the case of small consignments loaded with other goods.

(12.) At every station at which a train stops, the Guard must make a special examination of the vehicles containing any description of explosives or other dangerous goods, and must more especially examine the axle-boxes, and, if there is the least sign of heating, the vehicle must be detached, and the attention of the Station Master specially directed to it. Special care must be taken not to bring any light in close proximity to vehicles containing explosives or inflammable goods.

If it be necessary to detach, as unfit to travel a vehicle containing explosives or other dangerous goods at any point short of its destination, the Guard must advise the person in charge of the station or siding where the vehicle is detached in order that the necessary precautions may be taken by all concerned in dealing with the vehicle.

(13.) Before detaching at the end of the journey, or at exchange sidings, vehicles containing any description of explosives or dangerous goods, the Guard must call the special attention of a duly authorised person, and obtain his instructions as to the disposal of the vehicles.

(14.) At both the sending and receiving stations, vehicles containing any description of explosives or dangerous goods, or traffic of an inflammable nature referred to in clause (4), must not be placed within any of the Company's sheds or warehouses. On arrival at the receiving station such vehicles must be immediately separated from other vehicles.

When small lots of explosives or other dangerous goods or of traffic of an inflammable nature, which are loaded with other goods are received in sheds or warehouses they must be immediately removed from such buildings.

NOTES.—Explosives and other dangerous goods must not, except where special instructions are given to the contrary, be carried by trains conveying passengers.

Loose shunting of vehicles containing explosives is strictly prohibited.

VEHICLES CONTAINING EXPLOSIVES.

Not more than five vehicles containing explosives must be conveyed by any one train at any one time. Vehicles containing explosives or highly inflamable liquids or tank wagons containing compressed liquified gases must be marshalled as near the middle of the train as possible. Vehicles containing explosives and tank wagons containing compressed liquified gases must not be placed on the train near to vehicles containing inflammable liquids or other traffic of an inflammable nature.

At every station at which a train stops, the Guard must make a special examination of the vehicles containing any description of explosives or other dangerous goods, and must more especially examine the axle boxes, and, if there is the least sign of heating, the vehicle must be detached, and the attention of the Station Master specially directed to it. Special care must be taken not to bring any light in close proximity to vehicles containing explosives or inflammable goods.

If it be necessary to detach, as unfit to travel, a vehicle containing explosives or other dangerous goods at any point short of its destination, the Guard must advise the person in charge of the station or siding where the vehicle is detached in order that the necessary precautions may be taken by all concerned in dealing with the vehicle.

Before detaching at the end of the journey, or at exchange sidings, vehicles containing any description of explosives or dangerous goods, the Guard must call the special attention of a duly authorised person, and obtain his instructions as to the disposal of the vehicles.

---

*Note:— These instructions are liable to modification and amendment during the War Period and Trainmen should refer to the respective Companies' official publications.

14

A DRIVER & FIREMAN'S DUTIES

An engine driver has a highly responsible job. Not only is he in charge of an expensive locomotive and train, but it is often loaded with tons of valuable material, or hundreds of passengers. A simple mistake could cost thousands of pounds, or many lives. Not only would an accident to his train be costly in lives or materials, but might also involve another train.

A driver can never really relax, always listening for sounds indicating defects and keeping a good lookout for signals and obstructions. Keeping a good lookout is not always easy; cab windows, especially on large steam engines, are small and the view sometimes obscured by smoke or steam. Often he would gain a better sight by leaning out of the cab, unpleasant in wet or cold weather. Until about 1920 most cabs provided minimal shelter and seats for the crew were not general until about 1930.

A driver's main controls are the regulator, which admits steam to the cylinders, and the reverser. The latter, either worked by a lever or a screw reverser handle, controls the cut-off, so that once an engine is in motion, the steam can be used more expansively and thus save coal and his fireman's efforts. His third main control is the brake. Sanding gear, either steam or gravity fed, assists adhesion on a slippery rail.

In addition to attending to the fire and maintaining the correct water level, a fireman acts as his driver's second pair of eyes, helping him look out for signals and glancing back to ensure that the train is complete. He is responsible for keeping the footplate clean and tidy, damping down the coal dust. On a single line, the fireman collects and delivers the single line tablet, calling out the section to which it refers so that both he and his driver know it to be the correct one. The fireman is also responsible, under his driver's command, for screwing down the handbrake when a goods train is descending a gradient.

A driver often had a greater influence over a young fireman than his parents, for he was in his company longer. A swearing, drunken driver could pass these characteristics to his fireman, while a happy, sober driver could have a good influence on his young fireman. Some drivers were uncommunicative and drew a chalk line down the centre of the cab, saying, 'This is my side and that's yours', but a good driver helped his fireman, letting him drive occasionally and take a rest while he took over the shovel to keep his hand in.

DRIVER'S AND FIREMAN'S DUTIES.

The DRIVER and FIREMAN should—

Be with their engine at such time as the Locomotive Superintendent may require and satisfy themselves that the engine is in proper order.

To examine notices.

Ascertain from the notices posted for their guidance if there be anything requiring their special attention on the lines over which they have to work, and before leaving duty ascertain the time at which they are again required to be on duty.

Coal.

Coal, etc., to be safely stacked on engine.

Engines not to be left.

Engines not to be left without a man being in charge of it unless otherwise directed in the Rules, or it is absolutely necessary for them to do so, or the engine is in a siding and out of gear with the hand break hard on.

Smoke and steam from engines.

Arrange the fire so as to avoid any unnecessary emission of smoke particularly whilst standing at or passing stations, and prevent blowing off steam at safety valves as far as possible.

Fires, cinders, etc.

When passing through a tunnel refrain from throwing out fire, or cinders, also hot water as far as practicable, and exercise care in doing so at other places.

Leaving Footplate.

When the engine is in motion, trainmen must not expose themselves to danger by leaving the footplate unnecessarily for the purpose of going out on the engine framing or on top of the tender or bunker. Should, however, the Driver decide it is absolutely necessary that he should leave the footplate and does not consider it desirable to stop the train he must, before leaving, instruct his Fireman to keep a good lookout and observe the signals during his absence. Should it be necessary for the Fireman to leave the footplate while the engine is in motion, this must only be done by consent of the Driver.

Observations.

Observe signal boxes when passing them and in the case of trains not fitted throughout with the continuous brake, look back frequently during the journey, particularly when accelerating after speed has been reduced, to see that the whole of the train is following in a safe and proper manner (Rule 126).

The DRIVER should—

Articles to be taken.

Have with him a complete set of lamps, not less than 12 detonators, two red flags, a bucket when necessary, and such tools as may be ordered by the Locomotive Superintendent.

Lamps, discs, etc.

Before starting, see that the prescribed lamps, discs, or indicators, and destination boards where provided are exhibited and in good order, also that the lamps and indicators are lighted when necessary.

Conductor.

When not thoroughly acquainted with any portion of the line over which he has to work, obtain the services of a competent Pilotman.

To observe and obey signals.

Observe and obey all signals, whether the cause of the signal being shewn is known to him or not, and when owing to **fog, falling snow** or **other cause,** the fixed signals are not visible at the usual distance, use every precaution and **reduce speed if necessary,** especially in approaching stations or junctions, to enable train to be stopped at the signal should it be at Danger.

Look-out to be kept.

Keep a good look-out when the engine is in motion and sound the whistle when necessary.

Use of Whistle.

Sound the whistle as a warning when persons are seen on, or near to, the line on which his train is running ; also when unable to obtain a clear view of the line ahead owing to steam or smoke, as a warning to anyone who may be on the line, and when approaching or leaving a station where there is another train standing on the next adjoining line ; when approaching and passing any place where shunting operations are in progress on the next adjoining line or siding ; when entering and emerging from tunnels ; and frequently when passing through long tunnels. When approaching a junction, give the required junction whistle if the signals are at Danger.

Train not to move until signal is lowered.

When station work is completed, not to move his train towards the signal controlling the starting of trains from a platform, before it is lowered, except when specially ordered to do so by the Station Master.

Hose of water tanks.

After taking water from tanks or water-columns be careful to leave the hose or water crane clear of the running lines and properly secured.

Train not to foul running line.

Before moving his train on to, setting back from, or crossing, any running line see that proper signals are exhibited for the movement.

Engine not to foul points or crossings.

When bringing his engine to a stand in obedience to signals, the engine not to stand foul of the points or crossings of any other running line.

Regulation of speed.

Regulate the running of his engine to ensure punctual working, care being taken to avoid excessive speed. Special or relief train, not timed, must be run as nearly as practicable at the same rate of speed as corresponding trains shewn in the working time-table, and not to exceed such speeds unless under specific instructions. When running through junctions to or from lines diverging from the straight road, regulate the speed to ensure a steady passage for the whole train through the junction points and crossings.

Observe in all cases the speed restrictions shewn in the appendices or notices.

Fireman observing signals.

Have his fireman disengaged, as far as practicable, when approaching or passing a signal box, so that he also may keep a good look-out for signals ; he must also be, vigilant and cautious and **not trust entirely to signals.**

Starting and Stopping of trains.

Start his train carefully and proceed along the proper line, also stop his train with care, paying particular attention to the state of the weather, the condition of the rails and the gradient, as well as to the length and weight of the train. These circumstances must have due consideration in determining when to shut off power and to apply the brake.

Care in approaching stations.

Carefully approach stations at which his train is required to stop, and not to stop short of, or over-run, the platform.

Obeying instructions.

Obey the instructions of Station Masters.

Signal to reduce speed.

When a green hand signal is waved slowly from side to side by a Handsignalman, reduce speed to 15 miles an hour, or such other reduced speed as may be prescribed over the portion of the line to which such hand signal applies.

Fixed or hand signals during fog.

During fog or falling snow, keep a sharp look-out for the Fogsignalmen, who except as prescribed in first paragraph of clause (f) of Rule 91, will repeat the indications exhibited at the fixed signals shewing a **red, yellow,** or **green hand signal,** as the case may be, **held steadily.** When the fixed signals cannot be seen by the Driver on approaching them he must, in the case of a distant signal, unless he can see the Fogsignalman's hand signal, assume that that signal is at **Caution** and **proceed accordingly.** Where a stop signal is concerned he must, unless he can see the Fogsignalman's hand signal assume that the signal is at **Danger** and **stop his train immediately**.

Failure of block apparatus.

When informed by the Signalman that the block apparatus has failed and permission has been given for the train to go forward, **proceed cautiously** and not assume on approaching the signal box ahead that the fact of the signals being in the Clear position is an indication that the line is clear for his train (Rule 127).

FIREMAN'S DUTIES.

The FIREMAN should—

Look-out

When not necessarily otherwise engaged, observe and obey all signals and keep a good look-out all the time the engine is in motion (Rule 128).

Firing.

The following paragraphs contains a few practical hints culled from an official publication of a Main Line Company, which will be useful to Firemen. The principal points to be observed are as follows—

When a Fireman comes on duty and has examined the water level in the boiler and tested the water gauge cocks, his attention should then be given to the state of the firebox . He should, whenever possible, see that tube ends, brick arch and stays are clean, also that there is no leakage from either lead plugs, tubes, stays, etc. He should follow this up by opening the smokebox door, satisfy himself that there is no leakage at that end of the boiler, that the blast pipe and jet pipe, etc. are in order, that all ashes have been cleaned out and, finally, before gently closing the door, he should wipe its edge and the smokebox beading with a greasy cloth, bearing in mind that it is most essential to make an airtight joint, which materially assists in maintaining steam throughout the journey.

Having satisfied himself that the ashpan has been cleaned out and the firebars are in proper order, he can then take steps to make up his fire. Great care must be exercised in building up the fire in order to ensure a good supply of steam on the journey. A great deal depends upon the first layer of fire being well burnt through, as to add coal to a fire that is black on the top is to court trouble on the journey, so that every care must be taken in this direction. When the coal already put in the firebox is burnt through more should be added and the fire should be gradually built up until there is sufficient body of it, thickest in back corners and under the door, which method is usually satisfactory for the modern engine.

Coal is of various qualities and compositions, the greater part of it being carbon, the remaining portion composed of gases and ash. Some coals produce a clinker, which runs to the bars ; a good preventative of this is to scatter some limestone or broken fire brick (old brick arch) over the bars before making up the fire. The limestone or fire brick should be broken into pieces not larger than an average sized hen's egg. This not only keeps the metallic substance in the coal from coming in contact with and running to the bars, but it also makes the cleaning of the fire at the end of the journey much easier.

Very large lumps of coal should not be put into the firebox but should be broken to a reasonable size, care being taken not to make too much small or dust. It is easy to imagine what takes place when lumps of coal are deposited against the firebox side, or pushed forward against the tube plate ; holes are thus formed allowing cold air to pass through the fire and play upon the plates, setting up local contractions, while the other parts of the firebox are under expansion owing to the heat of the fire, and this inequality will cause the tube ends to leak and thick smoke will be given off.

The excessive use of fireirons on the journey is a bad practice ; it is, however, sometimes necessary when commencing the journey to run the pricker lightly through the fire and ease it—also when finishing the run it may be essential to use the bent dart to push the fire from under the door towards the front end in order to burn it down preparatory either to cleaning it or stabling the engine.

Every care should be taken when firing to avoid undue emission of smoke ; this should be the Fireman's first consideration. When too much smoke is emitted it means gases are being wasted, resulting in loss of heat and waste of coal, in addition to causing a public nuisance and complaints from the Health Authorities. The proper method of firing is to fire little and often, especially when using very small coal. To avoid the emission of black smoke from shunting engines, it has been found advantageous to fire alternate sides of the firebox ; by this means one half of the fire is kept in a bright state and consumes the smoke emitted from the fire at the other side.

Various quantities of air are required according to the thickness of the fire, and should be regulated by manipulating the damper and firehole door. Air will not flow freely through banks in the fire and combustion at these points will not be satisfactory. Large quantities of air will pass through the thinner parts of the fire and the unburnt gases arising from the banks may not receive a sufficient supply of air to enable them to be burnt, thus allowing gases to pass into the tubes in the form of smoke. Every Fireman should be aware that the passage of air through the damper and firebars causes rapid combustion of the heated fuel which gives off gases. These gases have to be supplied with air, which enters the firehole door and is directed under the brick arch by the deflector.

The brick arch prevents the gases from escaping unconsumed through the tubes and chimney in the form of black smoke, doing no useful work and choking up the tubes.

There are certain engines which require firing in a way peculiar to themselves. Some engines with horizontal firebars require a level fire ; others require the fire a little thicker at the back end; engines with sloping firebars have a tendency to draw the fire towards the tube plate, and great care must be exercised by quickly turning the shovel and directing the coal into the back corners and under the firehole door. If the fuel is allowed to be drawn off the fire shovel as it enters the firehole door, it will result in an accumulation against the tube plate.

It is inadvisable to commence firing when leaving a station. The Fireman should first satisfy himself that the train is following in a proper manner. When the engine has started the exhaust will begin to lift and liven the fire, which had settled down after the regulator was closed for making the stop, and then is the time to start firing. A distinct advantage is gained by waiting until the engine is notched up, in order that too much cold air is not admitted to the firebox through the firehole door, as would be the case if firing was taking place when the engine was in full travel.

15

A GUARD'S DUTIES

A guard is in charge of the train, while the driver is in charge of the locomotive.

A railway guard is a direct descendant of a Post Office mail coach guard. There were two types of train guard: passenger or goods. A passenger guard was normally under cover most of his working life, either at a platform, or in his brake compartment, whereas a goods guard might well be shunting in the open air. A passenger guard had intercourse with the public, whereas a goods guard normally only spoke to his fellow railwaymen. A passenger guard was in charge of luggage, parcels, mail and small animals, whereas a goods guard did not normally have such duties. All guards were responsible for giving the 'Right away' by whistle and green flag, or a lamp at night. Passenger guards travelled either in the brake compartment of a coach which also had passenger compartments, or else in a full brake which was given entirely to the use of the guard and parcels, etc.

All guards were expected to check that their driver was obeying signals and speed restrictions, and if necessary, applying the brake. A goods guard was required to assist with his train's braking and it was in his interest to ensure that the coupling between his van and the vehicle in front was kept taut in order to avoid undue bumps. Nevertheless, in his four-wheeled van he enjoyed a much less comfortable ride than his passenger counterpart. Some goods guards kept their own van and some carpeted it, making it a home from home. A goods guard was required to know the road well so that he could assist controlling the train on falling gradients.

In the event of an accident, or out-of-course stop, a guard is required to go back and protect his train with detonators and a red flag. In his Guard's Journal he is required to record the number of the engine, the name of its driver, details of the vehicles and load, and alterations to the consist as vehicles are attached and detached. Arrival and departure times at stations have to be noted, together with the cause of any delay.

GUARD'S DUTIES.

Every GUARD should—

Attendance.

Be in attendance at the place from which he is to start at such time as may be fixed, before the time appointed for the departure of his train.

Examination of notices.

Ascertain from the notices posted for his guidance if there is anything requiring his special attention, and before leaving duty ascertain the time at which he is again required to be on duty.

Kit.

Have with him a watch, and in his brake van a red and a green flag, not less than **12 detonators, a hand lamp, which must be lighted before passing through long tunnels,** after sunset and during fog or falling snow, and such other articles as may be ordered by the Operating Superintendent ; also, when working a Passenger train have a whistle and carriage key, and when working a Goods train have in his brake van a shunting pole and not less than **two sprags.**

Before starting train.

Satisfy himself before starting his train at the commencement of the journey that—

(1) the train is provided with necessary lamps ;

(2) all couplings between the vehicles are properly connected ;

(3) the continuous brake, where provided, is in working order, and all handbrakes are taken off ;

(4) the train is formed in accordance with instructions.

Travel in brake van.

He will travel in the brake van, except when required to travel in any other part of the train or upon the engine in the execution of his duty.

Examination of loads.

Examine the loading of vehicles attached on the journey, and if any become unsafe through displacement of the load he must at once have the load readjusted or the vehicle detached.

Braking.

Apply his brake when approaching, at too great a speed, a station at which the train is booked to stop.

Tail and side lamps.

When a vehicle is attached to, or detached from, the rear of a train at an intermediate station, see that the **tail lamp,** and **side lamps** where provided, are in their **proper places on the train.**

Attaching vehicles.

See that vehicles attached on the journey are placed in the proper position on the train.

Stoves in vans.

See that stove fire in van is extinguished before leaving the van unless the van has to be used again immediately, in which case a small fire may be allowed to remain, all necessary precautions being taken to avoid damage arising therefrom. Where gas or electricity is provided, turn this off before leaving the van.

Train journals.

When in charge of a train, forward to the proper official, at the end of his journey, a journal or journals containing the time of the running of his train, noting thereon every unusual circumstance, any detentions that may have taken place on the journey, and any error as to parcels, luggage or goods. In the event of any occurrence having taken place which might have involved the safety of the train or line, he must, in addition to the notes on his journal, make a special report thereof.

Guards travelling.

When travelling in a train other than that which he is appointed to work, if so instructed by a Station Master, render any assistance necessary in the working of the train, and obey any instructions received from the Guard in charge.

Assisting with luggage.

When waiting at stations assist with luggage, parcels, etc., to facilitate the despatch of trains (Rule 129).

PASSENGER TRAIN WORKING.

Every GUARD when in charge of a Passenger train should—

Before commencing journey.

Satisfy himself that the train is correctly labelled, and the emergency and first aid equipment, where provided, is intact ; also see that the doors of the carriages and other vehicles are properly closed and fastened ,and assist the station staff in this duty.

Unusual stoppage.

In the case of any unusual stoppage, request the passengers **not to alight** except when it is necessary for them to do so.

Brake Vans.

No unauthorised person to travel in a brake van or luggage compartment.

Attaching or detaching vehicles.

After a vehicle is attached or detached and before the train is again started see that the **couplings** between the vehicles concerned are **properly connected,** and that the hand brake on any vehicle which may have been attached is taken off. The Guard must see that the continuous brake, where provided, is in working order throughout the train.

Names of Stations.

Call out clearly the **names of the stations at** which the train stops during the journey, and at junction stations also announcing the **changes for connecting trains.**

Examination of Tickets.

Request the passengers to have their tickets ready at stations where tickets are examined or collected on the train, and also assist the ticket collectors by opening and closing the carriage doors; he must not, however, collect or examine tickets except under special instructions.

Passengers travelling irregularly.

Assist the staff at stations in preventing passengers travelling in a superior class or leaving the train for the purpose of re-booking by the same train to evade payment of the proper fare; also assist the staff generally in detecting fraudulent travelling (Rule 130).

GOODS TRAIN WORKING.

Every GUARD when in charge of a goods train should—

Starting and during journey.

Satisfy himself before the commencement of and during the journey, that all doors and sheets are securely fastened and the vehicles properly loaded, marshalled and coupled; also that the prescribed brake power is available, and in proper working order.

Applying brakes.

When travelling down a steep gradient, apply the rear hand brake to steady the train, but not to skid the wheels; also, where necessary, or when requested by the Driver, fasten down a sufficient number of wagon brakes before descending the gradient.

Delivery of train.

Unless instructions are given to the contrary, not leave the train until it has been delivered over to the Shunter, relief Guard or other authorised person (Rule 131).

16

BRAKES

Early steam locomotives often had no brake on the engine, one being provided only on the tender, so an emergency stop was effected by throwing the engine into reverse. Increasing loads and speeds of passenger trains demanded the introduction of continuous brakes which could be worked from the engine.

One of the most popular mechanical brakes was the Clark chain brake, whereby a friction-clutch on a brake van axle worked a windlass which tightened a chain operating brakes on adjoining vehicles. F. W. Webb modified the device and until around 1880 the Clark & Webb chain brake was the most reliable system.

Although hydraulic brakes proved powerful, there was a loss of fluid each time the hoses were coupled and uncoupled and the spilt oil was dangerous and expensive, while water could not be used because of the danger of freezing. It was realised eventually that using air was the answer, either compressed air, or the atmosphere acting against a partial vacuum.

There were three types of pneumatic brake. The cheapest was the 'simple' vacuum brake developed in the USA by James Young Smith. An ejector on a locomotive exhausted air from a pipe running throughout the train, a cylinder under each coach applying the brakes. Although powerful, it was slow to act and had the serious disadvantage that if a connecting pipe broke the brake was inoperative.

The second type was the automatic vacuum as improved by James Gresham, an English engineer who took out numerous patents concerning the vacuum brake. Either an ejector or a vacuum pump continuously maintained a vacuum in the train pipe to hold the brakes off. The brake was applied by destroying the vacuum in the train pipe, thus allowing the natural air pressure on one side of the cylinder to apply the brakes. It was safe because any breakage in the train pipe, perhaps caused by a vehicle becoming detached, would automatically apply the brakes on both portions.

Initially the automatic vacuum brake worked slowly as air had to pass along the train pipe. This problem was solved by the introduction of a direct admission valve which opened automatically when the train pipe vacuum was rapidly destroyed.

When a passenger pulls the communication cord in a coach it admits air to the brake pipe and applies the brake. The application is not so quick as to stop a train immediately and allows the driver, by means of the large ejector, to hold the brake off sufficiently long to enable the train to run clear of a tunnel, viaduct or other dangerous stopping place. The train cannot continue until the communication cord has been re-set. A 'butterfly' on the outside of a coach indicates the vehicle in which the cord has been pulled and the cord will be left hanging until re-set.

A development in the USA was the compressed air brake developed by George Westinghouse. Each locomotive has an air pump, air-pressure regulator and an air reservoir, while under each vehicle is an air reservoir, brake cylinder and triple valve. When the brake system is being charged, the triple valve vents the brake cylinder to the atmosphere and charges the reservoir until the pressure in the brake pipe and reservoir are almost equal. To apply the brake, a driver reduces the train pipe pressure and a valve isolates it from the reservoir and admits air from the reservoir to the brake cylinder in proportion to the reduction of pressure in the air pipe.

Although the Westinghouse brake is powerful and quick-acting, it has the disadvantage that, once applied, it cannot be eased off without fully releasing and then re-applying it. Until drivers realised this, accidents occurred when a driver released his brakes completely when trying to avoid stopping short.

The Caledonian, Great Eastern, London, Brighton & South Coast and North British Railways favoured the Westinghouse brakes, most other British railways choosing the automatic vacuum, so dual-fitted coaches had to be made available for certain through workings. In the post-Grouping era the Big Four standardised on vacuum brakes for locomotive-hauled stock.

THE VACUUM AUTOMATIC BRAKE.

GENERAL DESCRIPTION

This brake stops the train by the application of brake blocks to the tyres, in the same way as the brake blocks are applied by ordinary hand brakes. The levers, however, which apply the blocks, are moved by a piston working in a cylinder, the piston deriving its power from the **pressure of the atmosphere.**

It is continuous, each vehicle carrying its own brake cylinder which is connected to a pipe running from end to end of the train, and it is through this pipe that the action of the brake cylinders is controlled.

An ejector placed upon the engine exhausts the air out of the continuous pipe and cylinders, the brake is applied by the admission of air into the train pipe, and released by the withdrawal of the air through the ejector.

The brake can be applied by the Guard, and is self-acting in the case of an accidental parting of the train, or any damage happening to the brake itself.

It is instantaneous and direct in its action, and can be regulated to a nicety for easy stops, or to control the train on an incline.

THE ACTION OF THE BRAKE.

The engine having been coupled to the train, and the hose couplings connected between the tender and the train and also between the coaches, and the hose coupling at the end of the train having been placed upon the plug, the Driver admits steam to the small ejector, which soon exhausts the train pipe and cylinders, to a vacuum of from 20 to 24 inches, or the large ejector may be used if the vacuum is required to be obtained more rapidly. The small ejector must be kept at work **continuously** to maintain the vacuum.

To apply the brake the Driver moves the handle of the combination ejector in the direction marked " ON," thus admitting air to the train pipe and to the bottom of each cylinder, which lifts the pistons and so pulls the blocks to the wheels. The air cannot pass to the top of the piston, as it is prevented by the rolling ring. The power of the application is controlled by the amount of air let into the continuous pipe.

To release the brake, the handle must be returned to the " Running position," when the air let in to apply the brake will be removed through the small ejector; or it may be released more quickly by pushing the handle in direction marked " OFF " and so admitting steam to the large ejector.

The brake having been applied the pressure of the blocks on the wheels may be increased or diminished at pleasure without removing them, and also without reducing the full reserve power of the brake, which is always at command for an emergency stop.

Station stops should not be made by a violent application of the brake, but by a destruction of vacuum of, say, from 5 to 10 inches, which should be re-created slowly as the train comes to rest, by placing the handle in the " RUNNING POSITION ".

By having the vacuum nearly restored at the end of the stop, " jerking " is prevented, and the brake is released without the use of the large ejector.

To apply the brake quickly, the handle must be moved to the position marked " ON," thus fully opening the air valve.

The Guard can apply the brake by pressing down the handle of his valve, thus admitting air and applying the brake throughout the train, which it will stop even though the engine remains under full steam. When a rapid application is made by the Driver, the Guard's valve opens automatically, letting in air from the van, thus increasing the rapidity of the application, and it closes again after the brakes have been fully applied.

When it is desired to release the brake on coaches detached from the engine, the wire at either side of the vehicle must be pulled. The wire is attached to the lever of the release valve and, pulling the valve off its seat, allows the air to pass to the top of the piston, destroying the vacuum, and so releasing the brake. While this is being done a coupling must be left off the plug at the end of the train to allow the air to enter and destroy the vacuum.

GUARD'S VAN VALVE AND VACUUM GAUGE.

The Guard's Vacuum Gauge has one pointer indicating the amount of vacuum throughout the train.

The valve is fixed on the main train pipe and enables the Guard, by pressing down the handle, to apply the brake.

It also opens automatically when the Driver applies the brake suddenly, and admits air until the brake is fully applied.

The Valve has a small hole through its stem, and is secured at the top by a diaphragm to a small dome-like chamber, which chamber is exhausted when a vacuum is created in the train pipe. If a gradual application is made the vacuum in this chamber is destroyed as quickly as in the pipe, but when the brake is applied suddenly the vacuum beneath the valve is destroyed much quicker, and then the pressure of the atmosphere on the diaphragm lifts the valve, which remains open until the vacuum is destroyed in the dome-like chamber through the small hole, when it closes by gravity.

INSTRUCTIONS FOR WORKING THE VACUUM BRAKE.

Engine Driver's Instructions.

Before starting, the Driver must see that the gauge indicates at least 18 inches of vacuum, and that not less than this amount is maintained during the journey and while standing at stations. The vacuum is created by admitting steam to the small ejector, by means of the steam valve on combination ejector.

To apply the brake, move the handle on the combination ejector in the direction marked " ON ".

To release the brake move the handle on the combination ejector in the direction marked " OFF ".

In ordinary running position this handle must be in the " RUNNING POSITION ".

The small ejector steam valve must not be closed without first destroying the vacuum by applying the brake.

The ejector Drip Pipe and the Drip Valve on the pipe must be kept clear and free from dirt.

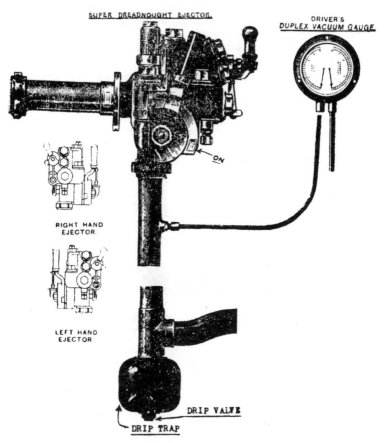

SUPER DREADNOUGHT EJECTOR.

DRIVER'S
DUPLEX VACUUM GAUGE

ON

RIGHT HAND
EJECTOR

LEFT HAND
EJECTOR

DRIP VALVE

DRIP TRAP

When in the shed, the hose pipes between the engine and tender should be uncoupled. If water be found in these pipes it is a sign that the back stop valves in the ejector require attention.

Guard's Instructions.

When the Guard has occasion to apply the brake he must press down the handle on the valve placed in his van. This admits air throughout the train pipe, and is only to be employed in cases of emergency. The valve in the van opens automatically when the brake is applied suddenly by the Driver, and ensures rapid action. The Guard must see that the gauge in his van records a vacuum of at least 18 inches and is maintained, or report otherwise to his Driver. He must also see that all hose-pipes between the carriages and engines are coupled together, and that the coupling on the last coach is properly placed on the plug.

Whenever the pipes between the vehicles are disconnected, the coupling must be placed upon the stop plug at the end of the vehicle.

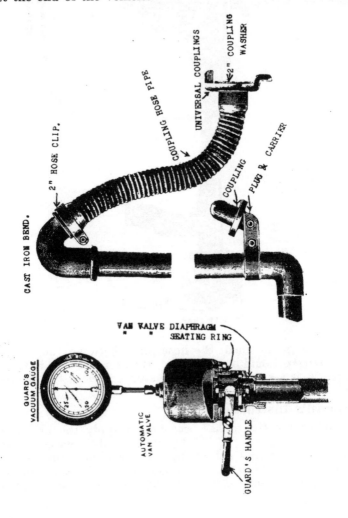

General Instructions.

To release the brake for shunting purposes (the engine having left the train, first see that the hose coupling at one end of the train is off the plug ; then pull the wire or cord fixed under the frame of each carriage. This admits air to the top side of the cylinder, and the brakes fall off by gravity.

To couple the pipes together, the Porter or other person doing this must take one in each hand and lift them sufficiently high to hook the bottom horns of the coupling together first, and, then by lowering them, place the top horns of the couplings in the slots.

To uncouple the pipes, simply lift them straight up when the lugs at the top will come out of the slots and the couplings will then separate and come apart.

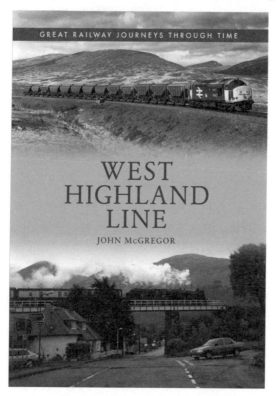

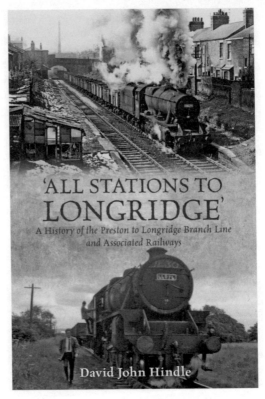

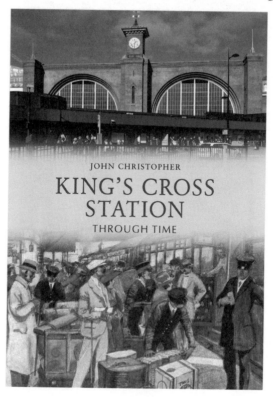

Also available from Amberley Publishing

A faithful facsimile of the 1935 original, updated with a new introduction and photo section

In the 1930s several of the railway companies published books to fulfil the public's interest. The GWR led the field, and *Track Topics* is a beautifully illustrated reproduction of the original 1935 publication. Illustrated with over 200 photographs and diagrams, it includes a new introduction by Brunel expert John Christopher plus a supplement section to bring the topics bang up to date.

£12.99 Paperback
Over 200 illustrations
288 pages
978-1-4456-2310-8

Available from all good bookshops or to order direct
Please call **01453-847-800**
www.amberleybooks.com

Also available from Amberley Publishing

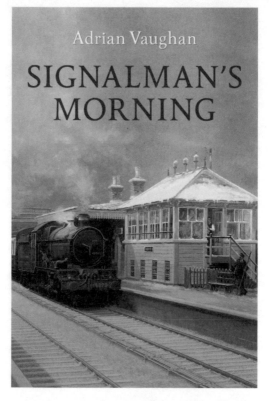

The first book in Adrian Vaughan's Signalman's trilogy:
a classic of railway literature

'A source of fascination to railway enthusiasts' *STEPHENSON LOCOMOTIVE SOCIETY*

In 1960, after 4½ years in the army, Adrian Vaughan joined the staff of Challow and became a signalman at Uffington a few months later. He was a signalman for fourteen years and an amateur footplateman for six. These are his memories, carefully remembered until, in 1978, he felt capable of writing them down on a 1942 vintage 'Imperial' typewriter, in a way to do justice to that wonderful epoch.

£16.99 Paperback
50 illustrations
192 pages
978-1-4456-0256-1

Also available as an ebook
Available from all good bookshops or to order direct
Please call **01453-847-800**
www.amberleybooks.com

Also available from Amberley Publishing

A narrative history of the most iconic railway company of the great age of steam

'Comprehensive and full of charming anecdotes' CHRISTIAN WOLMAR

'A very readable account of God's Wonderful Railway' *BBC WHO DO YOU THINK YOU ARE MAGAZINE*

The initials 'GWR' conjure an evocative picture of a Brunswick green locomotive hauling tea-and-cream- coloured coaches through a verdant West Country landscape. But the GWR was not just engines and trains. In this comprehensive history, Colin Maggs, one of the country's foremost railway historians, tells of other, perhaps less well-known aspects of the company's history.

£20.00 Hardback
118 illustrations (31 col)
352 pages
978-1-4456-1277-5

Available from all good bookshops or to order direct
Please call **01453–847–800**
www.amberleybooks.com

The third book in Adrian Vaughan's Signalman's trilogy:
a classic of railway literature

Signalman's Nightmare is the third volume of Adrian Vaughan's memories of his career on the Western Region of British Railways. The book begins in 1962 at Challow and starts with a confession of his terrible contravention of the regulations brought about by an intense desire not to delay a passenger train. For three years he worked at Uffington, which was the interface between the new signalling systems, centred on Reading 'Panel'. He tells of how Western Region permitted situations to arise that contravened the semaphore signalling regulations – and what he did about it.

£16.99 Paperback
192 pages
978-1-4456-0258-5

Also available as an ebook
Available from all good bookshops or to order direct
Please call **01453–847–800**
www.amberleybooks.com

*The second book in Adrian Vaughan's Signalman's trilogy:
a classic of railway literature*

In *Signalman's Twilight*, the second part of his trilogy, Adrian continues the story of his railway life in rural
West Berkshire, moving from Uffington signal box to that at Challow early in 1962. *Signalman's Twilight*
recalls the openness of the railway and the skill and commitment of the railwaymen. Adrian describes
how he tried single-handedly to save Challow station only to earn a severe reprimand from high
authority.

£16.99 Paperback
70 illustrations
192 pages
978-1-4456-0257-8

Also available as an ebook
Available from all good bookshops or to order direct
Please call **01453-847-800**
www.amberleybooks.com